ETHICS AND THE COMMUNITY OF GOD

Other Titles by the Same Author

Post-Colonialism Subalterns and Community (2015)
Introducing Post-Modernism and Post-Colonialism (2013)
Contextual Issues: Theological, Ethical and Missiological Responses (2011)
Christian Ethics: Issues and Insights (2007)
Human Rights: Concepts and Perspectives (2002)

About the Author

Rev. Dr. M. Stephen hails from Kottayam (Kerala, India) is a writer, orator and author. He has authored around 30 books in Malayalam and English. He received his B.A. and MA (in English Literature) from Kerala University, B.D. (UBS, Pune) and M.Th. (UTC, Bengaluru) from Serampore University (West Bengal), and Doctorate (Th.D) from Dharmaram Vidyakshetram: Pontificial Athenaeum of Philosophy and Theology, Bengaluru. He is a theological teacher and teaches theology and ethics at Faith Theological Seminary, Manakala, Adoor, Kerala. The famous publishers such as 'Concept', 'Serials' and ISPCK have published his books. *Human Rights*: *Contextual Issues*, *Christian Ethics: Issues and Insights*, and *Introducing Post-Modernism and Post-Colonialism* are published by Concept, Delhi.

Ethics and the Community of God

Dr. M. STEPHEN

CONCEPT PUBLISHING COMPANY PVT. LTD.
NEW DELHI - 110 059

ISBN: 978-93-5594-161-9

First Published 2022

Published and Printed by

Concept Since 1974

Concept Publishing Company Pvt. Ltd.
A/15-16, Commercial Block, Mohan Garden
New Delhi-110059 (India)
T: +91-11-4110 1460
E: publishing@conceptpub.com, W: www.conceptpub.com

Cataloging in Publication Data--Courtesy: D.K. Agencies (P) Ltd. <docinfo@dkagencies.com>

S̲t̲t̲īphan, Eṃ., author.
Ethics and the community of God / Dr. M. Stephen.
pages cm
Includes bibliographical references and index.
ISBN 9789355941619

1. Christian ethics. 2. Ethics in the Bible. 3. Church and social problems. 4. Bible--Criticism, interpretation, etc. I. Title.

LCC BJ1251.S74 2022 | DDC 241 23

INTRODUCTION

This book '*Ethics and the Community of God*' has reflection on current social, Biblical and theologico-ethical issues. It deals with transparency, justice, suffering, mission, education, prophets, Jubilee and nation of Israel. It also substantially deals with the crises in ethics which appears in the form of double morality. The political struggle of Martin Luther King Jr. is also discussed in this book.

The witness of nation of Israel among nations, the role of prophets in social justice, the ethical dilemma, and different common social issues are discussed in this book. Hope this book will enable us to examine ourselves to evolve a transformed community. The community of God should have a public witness in the morally corrupt society.

Christian witness involves the life of integrity and transparency. We should address the questions of the powerless and work for their emancipation. It is important to have an other regarding life and to stand for the dignity and rights of the poor. The prime importance should be given to the integral liberation of the marginalized in mission. It is very significant to listen to the voices of the marginated people and to make positive response to them. Hope this book may provide insights to reflect meaningfully on the issues around and to take adequate measures to resolve them.

Rev. Dr. M. Stephen
B.A. B.D., M.A. M.Th., Th.D.
Puthenparambil, Poovanthuruth P.O.,
Kaduvakulam, Kottayam, Kerala, India

CONTENTS

SECTION A

CHRISTIAN REFLECTIONS ON CURRENT ISSUES

CHAPTER I

LIFE OF INTEGRITY AND TRANSPARENCY

Transparency is the prerequisite for a life of integrity. What is lacking today is the transparency. The objects are classified into three — transparent, translucent and opaque. Light goes through the transparent objects without any kind of hindrance. The object like glass is very transparent, and the objects like wood or stone are opaque.

Transparency is essential for a life of integrity. Transparency is related to truth, righteousness, holiness and goodness (Phili. 4:8). Transparency means living in the light. We are asked to live in the light as God is also transparent in nature (1 John 1:5-7). Life of integrity and life of transparency are almost synonymous. If we are after evil we are not transparent. The evil is against integrity and transparency. We are to lead a holy or moral life in the context of evil. The evils are to be identified and respond to them. A transparent life is a responsible and responsive life. The evil is to be challenged and never compromise with it.

- We are the children of light, so we are to live in light and not in darkness. Our attitudes, perspectives and actions are to be transparent. The deceptive behaviour, exploitation and oppression are against transparency and integrity. Our attitudes and actions should bring good for others. We are to act as the light in the world, as Jesus our master is the true light of the world. Jesus was demanding a radical transparency in our attitudes through the Sermon on the Mount (Matt. Chapters 5-7). He seeks a life of integrity in relation to our attitude towards sex, money and relationships with others.

Jesus, in the Sermon on the Mount, asked the audience to be meek, holy, merciful and peace-makers. He advocated for a transparent relationship in the community for the harmonious co-existence. Life of Jesus was transparent as He was keeping up the integrity as leading a life based on holiness, love, mercy and service. He had a very exemplary life on earth. He was even willing to sacrifice his life for the good of others which shows his integrity.

The prophets of God have a life of transparency and integrity. They were the forth tellers. They were straightforward people. They were never intimidated to tell the truth. They had kept up the ideal of transparency. They dared to challenge the social evils found in the form of moral laxity, exploitation and oppression. Prophet Nathan was having the courage to confront King David as he had done injustice to Uriah. Elijah has the boldness to tell the truth to Ahab, as he was doing injustice to Naboth. For the sake of transparency and integrity, the prophets were willing to risk their life.

The prophets stood for justice or fair relationship. Prophet Amos had a vision of justice which is to be rolled like water. The moral degradation in the form of sexual immorality, bribery and other forms of corruption was questioned by prophets. They were transparent as they revealed without fear the message they have received from the Lord. They stood for the formation of a community based on justice and Shalom.

Transparency is important in our attitude and treatment to others. How we value others is very crucial over here. Recognizing the identity, dignity and rights of others, especially the oppressed and dehumanized ones is essential to the concept of transparency. The manipulations and all sorts of exploitations are against transparency. The pyramidal structures are very clever in using deceptive methods to keep the powerless away from their privileges and rights. Transparency is kept aside in order to uphold the caste system, patriarchy and capitalism by the dominant forces. This is to be challenged.

We should have transparency to respond to the evil social system which supports the oppression, disempowerment and inhumanity. The evil has to be named and challenged without intimidation. Dietrich Bonhoeffer had the transparency to name Adolf Hitler as anti-Christ. The transparency does provide courage to challenge the forces that enslave us.

CHAPTER II

THE CHALLENGE OF EMPOWERMENT

Empowerment is the centre of discussion in this century. Those who are dehumanized, oppressed and humiliated are seeking empowerment. The affirmation of freedom, identity, dignity and rights are inevitable for the empowerment as it is a liberative process.

The dominant class and caste do not like the empowerment of the poor and powerless. They are for exploiting and oppressing the subaltern people. The education, health care, employment, land, shelter, food and human rights are the essential ingredients of empowerment. The dominant groups are trying to disempower the poor, the women, children, dalits, tribes, people with disabilities, transgenders and the other marginated groups. The powerful are leading a luxurious life at the expense of the powerless. They use the powerless as their employees for cheap labour. In India, it is reported that, 95 per cent of the people are not having even six lakh rupees in their hand, but on the other hand 5 per cent of the people are rich who are holding crores of rupees and even more than these amounts. There are rich who holds 100-600 crores rupees. This is the paradox in the Indian context. The powerless are highly marginated, and the powerful are enjoying life at the maximum.

Millions of people in India and other Asian countries are landless poor, slum-dwellers, migrants, refugees and street-dwellers. There are many who found their shelter near railway tracks, bus stations and under bridges and big trees. Their identity as a citizen or security or welfare are being challenged. They live as 'no people'. Their life is miserable. They live in most unhealthy situation and their life is insecure.

The violence against the poor and powerless is a common scene in India today. The dignified survival of the women, dalits, tribal people, children and the transgender is in question. The transgenders are facing extreme forms of alienation and oppression. They are mistreated by the men, policemen, and the authorities. Their privileges are also denied. The family members consider them as a curse or burden. The society do not accept their identity and rights. They are undergoing psychological disturbance and insecurity. So they are to be empowered.

The oppression against women and children appear in the form of forced labour and sexual abuse. They are the instruments of ill-treatment like dalits and tribes as they are also the most alienated and powerless people. The dalits are born as bond-slaves and tribal people are also made powerless and oppressed. They are also forcefully evacuated from their habitat to make them landless and powerless. The powerful ones are using deceptive means to curb the emancipation, empowerment and liberation of the dalits, tribes, women, children and the poor. Unless these disempowered have access to the income generating resources their empowerment is not possible.

The slogan of Dr. Ambedkar 'educate, agitate and organize' is very important at this juncture for the emancipation of the powerless. The empowerment of the marginated is possible only through the organized struggles. The systemic violence is so strong that the structure does not permit the poor to come up. The powerless are victimized by the powerful for their advantage. This can be challenged only through the movement of the subaltern people.

The feudalistic and evil structures were trying to exploit and disempower the subaltern people which was being challenged by the prophets. The prophets were siding the empowerment of the poor. Jesus and his movement was challenging the structures of oppression and worked for the empowerment of the poor and marginalized. It was a dynamic process of liberation. The capital-intensive structures were challenged by prophets and Jesus in order to form a community of the empowered. This process of empowerment was continuing in the early Christian community through the work of the Holy Spirit (Acts. 1:8). Through the work of the Holy Spirit, the communities were renewed and reformed as they empowered the disempowered.

It is important to note that the Christian community today has to respond to the issues of the disempowered. Michel Foucault talks about the sharing of the power to the marginated and questioned the centring of power. The church has to involve in the activities which would empower the poor. The Christians also have the responsibility to join hands with the organizations which would deeply involve in the process of empowerment. We have to join the mission of Jesus (Lk. 4:16-21) to empower the disempowered in the society to form a new society which uphold the values of the Kingdom of God.

CHAPTER III

A CRY FOR RESTORATION

The words such as restoration, reconciliation and redemption are related to liberation. Restoration is the need of the hour. Restoration has personal, social and cosmic dimensions. It includes the spiritual renewal and structural transformation. In all dimensions of human life the restoration is inevitable.

The Israelites cried out for their restoration, while they were captives in Egypt and Babylon. As they were in oppressive condition they cried out to God for their liberation. They wanted to be redeemed from slavery to return to their homeland. While they were in Babylon, they asked God to forgive the sins of their community, as they understood that their captivity is caused by their injustices. The people of Judah invoked God to remember them in their pathetic condition. Their constant prayer can be summarized as 'restore us O' Lord'.

God always looks for the repentance of the people as a prerequisite for restoration. When Adam and Eve had their fall and yielded to sin, they were alienated from God. It resulted in the alienation of the whole humanity from God. A restoration from the fallenness was done by Jesus Christ through his cross. Jesus' incarnation was God's design to restore the humanity to God. Restoration means reinstatement of what is lost or fallen.

There are a vertical and horizontal dimensions in restoration. We have to restore to God and to the humanity. In the divided and broken world, the restoration of love, peace and justice are significant. The oppressive and divisive forces are at work in the world. The caste system is used as tool by the dominant class to oppress the poor. The justice is denied to them. Their rights are curtailed. The marginated groups are exploited and victimized so they are to be restored. The oppressive forces took the form of caste system, racism, fascism, patriarchy, colonialism and neo-colonialism. Challenging the evil forces is essential for the restoration. Restoration of the people from the discriminations to dignity and justice is to be promoted.

The restoration is found in a holistic sense in the book of Leviticus in the form of jubilee (Lev. 25). There was spiritual, social and economic restoration. The land was restored so also they were restored from slavery. Jubilee was a challenge to feudal system. Another challenge to capitalistic system is the understanding of koinonia (Acts. 2:42-47; 4:32-35). The creation is also looking forward to the restoration of humanity (Rom 8:22-25), which in turn restores the whole of creation. Along with man, the creation also needs the restoration. In the name of modernism, development and consumerism, the human beings have tortured the nature.

The restoration is quite related to the Kingdom of God. Entering into the Kingdom of God means restoration. The "new birth" (John 3: 1ff) means a restoration to God and the entrance into the Kingdom of God. There is also a millennial or messianic rule promised which is a radical dimension of restoration. Millennial rule is the radical realization of the Kingdom of God where justice and peace prevail. The ultimate form of restoration is found in the "new earth and new heaven" (Rev. 22), where everything is restored to God.

CHAPTER IV

THE CHRISTIAN VIEW OF SUFFERING

Suffering is a common element for humanity as it is part and parcel of the whole of humanity's experience. Suffering in one sense or another is unavoidable to all human beings. This is a very crucial crisis that all creation has to encounter each moment. Almost all religions of the world understand suffering as an evil. For Hinduism it is an illusion or '*maya*'. It is in the realm of the unreal. In Buddhism, suffering is caused by desire. One has to transcend the desire in order to overcome the suffering. '*Dukha*' is universal in the understanding of Buddhism.

Suffering can be explained as pain. It can be physical pain, mental agony or social problems. The physical wounds or illness cause suffering, the psychological disturbances can cause suffering. Suffering affirms the presence of evil in the society.

The problem of evil is a serious issue in theodicy. Theodicy is God's affirmation of good or justice in the context of the challenge of evil. The entrance of sin has caused all suffering in the world. This is well portrayed by Bible in the book of Genesis (Chapter 3). Man, the creation of God, had rebelled against the creator. It is depicted that the evil force (Satan) had came in the form of a serpent in the beautiful garden of Eden, where Adam and Eve, the first parents stayed happily. By violating the Commandments of God, they yielded to the temptations of the evil force and fell into sin. The disobedience caused estrangement from God. They lost their dignity and status before God. God's indictment came upon them. They lost their glory, they were deprived and they became 'naked'. Literally and spiritually they were naked before the divine.

According to the Bible, man was created in the image of God (Gen. 1:27, 28). They were right before God. They were sharing God's holiness and righteousness. There was no darkness in them. There was no sin in them. The sin did lead man more finite. The suffering also entered the world as the sin entered the world. Man was above sin and suffering when he was created, but later because of disobedience they were yielded to suffering. Man was deprived in the status, dignity and their relationship with God. Man had to flee from the presence of God as they were fallen into the trap of sin. Sin had made man corrupt.

No human being can transcend the sin and suffering by his own efforts. The sin and suffering caused by original sin is a universal or perennial suffering. The sickness, death and other forms of suffering are common to the whole humanity. These sufferings have become quite natural for the whole human beings. These can be also punitive or a penal suffering. This suffering comes as a penalty to the violation of truth or overruling God's commandment (Roman 5:12). This is visible in the whole creation. If we analyse the case of David, the King, it is found that he violated the commandments and had to undergo the penal suffering. He was going against God's rule very deliberately and was reaping the consequences (2 Sam. 12:ff). The consequence of sin followed him.

There is also purgative or purificatory suffering—suffering for purification; this can come as an aspect of disciplining person or to modify a person. In the case of Job, it was clear that the intention was to purify him. He was tested to undergo the suffering so that he might win in the suffering. He had to undergo very intense form of suffering. He lost his children, cattles and property. His wife was blaming him. He was accused by his friends and was induced to become an atheist. They asked him to reject God. They did not see any rationale in this suffering, but he saw God as the vindicator of justice. He did believe that he would be purified and come out as purified gold. Of course, he did overcome the test and became a man of experience. He won the game. He realized the greatness of God and the divine providence.

In the case of Job, it is clear that the suffering he had undergone was for manifesting the glory of God. It is to reveal the glory of God. In the case of Daniel and his friends, it is said that, God himself intervened in the cases of suffering and persecutions. Daniel and his friends stood firm for the cause of God, determined to suffer the consequences, but God never left them alone. He was with them. They did see the presence of God in their struggles. So they were not afraid of the challenges of the authorities.

Jesus was always compassionate to those who are suffering. He healed and restored them. He was restoring the whole of humanity. His healing was holistic (John 5:1 ff). He raised the dead and wiped out the tears of the people (John. 4:50). Jesus said that in certain cases, suffering is for the glory of God (John 9:1-3) in the instance of the blindman, Jesus clearly stated that he is blind not because of the sins of anyone of his parents or forefathers, but to manifest the glory of God. In the miracle of raising the dead Lazarus, Jesus implicitly said that it was for revealing this glory. Certainly God was glorified through that instance (John 10:39-40).

There are cases in which we are trained through suffering. Bible states that the loved ones are disciplined by God (Heb. 12. 5ff). There is a fine depiction of this found in the parable of the wine (John 15). The branches are pruned to bear more fruit. It is interesting to note that though they are bearing fruit, they are pruned to have more fruit. This suffering is to make us more equipped so that one becomes more effective. There is also punitive aspect. The branches which are not bearing fruit are cut off. It is a penalty for the barrenness. The suffering that is intended to discipline is very creative and useful. The good God permits the righteous also to suffer to discipline and purify them. So there is no question in the issue of 'why righteous suffer?' The righteous suffer for good.

The vicarious suffering is another important aspect of suffering. This is a suffering on behalf of the other. One of the examples we found in the *Old Testament* is the 'suffering servant' in the book of Isaiah (Chapters 52 and 53). It is depicted as vicarious sufferings. It can be also called as propitiatory suffering. It is the suffering for the expiation of sins. In the *Old Testament*, sacrifices were offered to propitiate the sins of persons. The animals were sacrificed on behalf of the persons to expiate sins. They suffer for the cause of humanity.

The perfect example of vicarious suffering is found in Jesus Christ, son of God. He died for the sins of the humanity. He suffered so that the whole of universe can be restored. Apostle Paul states that Jesus Christ reconciled the humanity to God as he suffered (died) for the sins of the humanity (2 cor. 5:19-21). His suffering was vicarious one. He was accused and was made a shame as he suffered on the cross. It was a sacrificial suffering.

The Bible also clearly states that all Christians are to suffer for Christ's sake (1 Pet 4:15-16; 2:20-21). We are called to suffer for Christ. Bonhoeffer, the German theologian, said 'when Christ calls a man, he bids him come and die'. This is the cost of discipleship for him. It does mean that we are called to sacrifice our life for Christ's sake. A Christian must be ready for martyrdom.

Suffering is an inevitable element for all humanity, including Christians. There is suffering for good and suffering for bad. Vicarious suffering of Jesus Christ brings good to humanity. The suffering for purification through a disciplining process always does have positive effect. And it is quite essential to suffer as Christians.

Christians have a hope. The hope is that there is a world in which there is no tears and suffering. God will ultimately create a new heaven and earth, where there is peace and life (Revelation chapters 21-22). Our hope is that we are going to overcome the death and sufferings. We already realize this through Christ who carried away our sins and sufferings.

CHAPTER V

A LIBERATING VISION

God is the liberator. The Bible is the message of liberation. The spirit of liberation is found all through the Bible. God loves the whole mankind so he plans to liberate them from the clutches of unfreedom and oppression. The plenitude of God's plan of liberation is made realized through Jesus Christ, the supreme liberator.

In Latin America, the Biblical vision of Justice, Equality and Liberation is captured by the Basic Christian communities. They could see the inhuman situation around them. The realities of the context are known to them quite well. Centuries long oppression which dehumanizes the Latin American marginated is on the focus of their thinking. They learned the Bible and received the core message of the Bible. It was nothing but the activity of God's liberation for the oppressed.

What is the ultimate and total message of the Bible? Transformation of mankind and the whole cosmos is the intention of God. The total liberation includes the liberation of mankind and the whole of creation. The renewal of the cosmos is the message of the Bible. The new earth and new heaven is the final vision about the cosmos that Bible provides. The liberating vision includes the liberation of mankind and the creation (Rom. 8:18-23). The cosmic redemption is the main focus of the Bible.

The Kingdom of God has two dimensions: the present and the future. While discussing the concept of the Kingdom of God, wolfhart Pannenberg asserts that the aspirations for the other world will inspire us to transform the present. The responsibility of a Christian is to receive the vision of humanization as it is the integral part of the message of salvation. A vision is the motivating factor. It stirs us up. It is the spur which enables us to realize the urgency of our mission. The kingdom of God affirms justice, equality and dignity of men and women. The selfish interests have no place in the Kingdom of God. There are several 'construction companies' in the field for building up the kingdom. But the kingdoms that they build are their own and not God's. They are self-centred rather than God-centred.

The values of the Kingdom of God included the liberation of the poor, the dalits, the women and the preservation of the eco-system. There are Christians who believe that Bible has a vision which accepts the inferiority of women, oppression of the dalits and the violence over the eco-system. We should know that it is a distorted understanding. The Biblical vision and the values of the kingdom do affirm the integrity of the whole creation and the equality and dignity of all human beings.

We should be liberated from our short-sightedness. We need a macrocosmic vision rather than a microcosmic vision. The vision that Apostle Peter received was a transforming vision (Acts. 10). It was a vision that furnishes the radical message of the Bible. Regardless of the caste, colour and gender, everyone is equal in God's sight. It was a liberating vision that discloses the fact that in God's community no one is inferior to anyone. It reveals the unity, love and harmony of the whole mankind. The dividing walls among the human beings is caused by the selfishness of human beings.

Apostle Peter had a truncated vision, but that was corrected by the vision that he received. But there are churches which still hold the non-liberated vision of Peter. The discriminations in the name of caste, colour, gender and race are the clear examples for this. The non-liberated vision of Peter was part of 'helicopter christology' (S.J. Samartha). S.J. Samaratha proposed the ideas like 'helicopter christology' (Christology from above) and 'bullock-cart christology' (christology from below). Our theology should be a water-buffalo theology or Minjung theology, since it comes from the experience of the people in the Third World countries. It is important to develop a 'bullock cart christology' a theology or christology that integrates the experience of the poor. Our theology should have a liberating vision as against the *status quoic vision* of classical theologies. Our vision should capture the experience of the poor. Their experiences of suffering have to be the theme of our doing theology. Our liberating vision has to inspire us to emancipate the weak, down trodden and the poor.

The experience of poor is nothing but unemployment, suffering, oppression, exploitation, sickness, malnutrition and poverty. A liberating vision is important in doing theology. A liberating vision cannot accommodate the theories (e.g. prosperity theology) and the life style of the affluent. A liberating vision is not after an opulent life-style. It rejects the luxurious way of life. A liberating vision is needed to work for the liberation of the poor and oppressed who are struggling for their survival.

CHAPTER VI

SOLIDARITY IS THE NEED OF THE HOUR

The Latin word 'Solidaire' means unity. It stands for mutual dependence and holding together. It indicates the strong bond between persons or groups for a special cause. The words such as 'unity' and 'partnership' are related to solidarity and it has socio-political overtones. In the secular world 'solidarity' is used for the unity of people which forms as a movement for revolutionary action. It is an action centred unity.

Unity or solidarity is a major concern in the churches and the society. In order to maintain solidarity, the building up of proper relationship is very essential. The egoism, hatred and competition can ruin the solidarity. Love, brotherhood and tolerance can promote solidarity. The spirit of unity and fellowship were the major concerns of Apostle Paul (Phili 2:2;4:2). Unity within the members of 'ecclesia' was given utmost importance by the Apostles. One of the most important aspect of the early church and the work of the Holy Spirit was 'Koinonia' or solidarity that is centred around caring and sharing. It was a symbol of deep sense of unity.

Solidarity entertains the concern for others. We should have solidarity as we have sensitivity to the people and their issues. Our solidarity should not be limited to the Christian community alone. This solidarity should be a wider one as we relate to the cause of the common man. The civil society is one of the best example of the wider dimension of solidarity as it stands for justice and anti-corruption. The social movements (e.g. Ecological movements, women movements, anti-nuclear movement, land struggles) are also the best examples of human solidarity. They stand firm for the common causes of humanity, especially the subaltern people. God always has solidarity with the poor and marginalized. The Exodus even reflects God's Solidarity with the oppressed as God dynamically involves in the liberation of the subaltern people.

Jesus had solidarity with the Father, the disciples, and the people who are marginalized (Jn. 17). It was an ecumenical and subaltern solidarity as Jesus was concerned of the 'other' who are very significant in the post-colonial and post-modern thinking. Solidarity for the sake of Gospel involves solidarity with the poor and marginalized to share the good news through praxis. More than 65 per cent of Indians are poor. They constitute the lepers, slum-dwellers, migrants and landless bond-slaves. Our mission should not be reduced to mere charity, but it should be a liberative solidarity. The dalits, tribes, victimized women, children and other oppressed groups such as transgenders are to be empowered in order to be liberated from the yoke of oppression. The missiological dimension of solidarity has to inspire us to redeem the alocholics and narcotics, and to make peace in the situation of broken families and also to serve the differently-abled people. The understanding of solidarity should also enable us to identify with the neglected one.

Our solidarity will be lost as we dehumanize others. When we use violence against others in the form of sexual assault, injustices, or the use of nuclear and chemical weapons, the human solidarity is in a threat. Solidarity involves the tasks of incarnating into the lives of others who are suffering. It involves the act of transformation. It is the sharing of our resources and life of others. A real solidarity is risky as Jesus had a solidarity with the humanity on the cross to liberate them.

The real clue to solidarity is found in God himself. There is a strong bond or solidarity is found in Triune God as the oneness is shown. The solidarity and love in trinity is well re1flected as God himself incarnated in order to liberate the humanity. The missiological dimension of solidarity is found in Trinity as Jesus Christ has taken the human form, the enfleshment.

If God has solidarity with everyone as Jesus loved the humanity regardless of colour, caste, race or gender, it is important that we should have a dynamic solidarity with subalterns. Apostle Paul had seen this live solidarity as there is unity of different categories of people (Gal. 3:28). The unity or solidarity means we have to overcome the unequal relationships. Martin Luther King Jr. , the leader of the American Civil Right Movement, has pictured this solidarity in his famous speech (1963) 'I have a dream' that there is solidarity between the blacks and whites one day. He said in his famous Washington speech "I have a dream that one day on the red hills of Georgia the sons of former slaves and the sons of former slave-owners will be able to sit down together at a table of brotherhood."

Solidarity is dynamic, and praxis-oriented as it is deep rooted in love, unity and fraternity. It provides space for a unified action to overcome the discrimination in the name of caste, race, colour, gender and status. It upholds the dignity, rights and identity of all especially the victimized and subalterns.

CHAPTER VII

PERFECTION IS THE ETHICAL OPTION

Perfection is a process. Everyone is trying to attain the perfection. Perfection and maturity are the goals set by God, but every Christian is not particular about it. Jesus said, "you should be perfect as the Father is perfect" (Mt. 5:48). There is a process of regeneration, sanctification and glorification. Glorification is a later event. We should have a holy, sincere and transparent life before God, human beings, and the whole creation. Creation is also integral part of humanity to which you should not do sin or injustice. 'Be perfect' is a command which also has ecological implications.

Christian perfection is very much stressed by Weslyan theology. Whether the sinless perfection is possible on this terrestrial life is a debatable issue. But the real question is whether a Christian can have a insincere, unfaithful, arrogant, opaque life? There are Christians who involve in deception, undermining and swindling (of money) without even a prick of conscience. It is also found that the so called 'holy' and 'perfect' play tricks to dehumanize others. For some of them sexual chastity is not a serious issue. They dare to involve in sexual immorality. Justification of any form of imperfections through our own word or deed will lead to judgment.

There are several superfluous Christians who are not particular about the Christian principles, as they believe that perfection can be achieved only in a life hereafter, so they involve in every evil and justify it. Some Christians only look into individual or personal dimension of perfection and they fail to relate to social dimension of it. An integral vision is needed to have a perfect view on perfection. It is true as Tolstoy stated that there are so many people to make the world good, but they never try to become good. This is the sad story. In Bonhoeffer's view Christ formation is an important dimension. Christ should form in us. Apostle Paul also affirms the fact that Christ has to form in us (Gal. 4:19). In the process of perfection, Christ formation plays a significant role.

As Christians we cannot have an isolated exclusive life of perfection. There are pillar saints like Simon Stylus who hardly relate with people as they think that relating with people might lead to unholiness and unchastity. This is a very shallow understanding about perfection and holiness. Being perfect means, how we are able to relate meaningfully with others even in our commitment and responsibility to others.

We should be aware that the forceful acquiring of land from the poor, exploitation of resources, evacuation of people from their original habitat in the name of development, irresponsible tapping of resources like water, coal and minerals, pollutiong the water, soil and air by carbon monoxide, carbon dioxide, sulphur dioxide, chloro-fluoro-oxides, the chemical waste, nuclear waste and human waste are all sin to humanity and to the whole of creation. Sin also has an ecological dimension. Misuse or irresponsible use of energy is also sin, so it is keeping away from perfection. Eco-friendly, poor-friendly, victims-friendly (the victims such as poor women, children, dalits and tribes) attitudes are a sign of perfection. Victimizing is sin, and supporting the victimization in the name of caste, colour, gender and class is a grave sin, which is a hindrance to perfection.

The attempt to become perfect is found everywhere. The people are creating a public space, even a virtual space (cyber space) to respond to the forces of evil or imperfection. Perfecting the society from the injustices, exploitation, the human right violations, poverty and corruption is an organized attempt today. The action groups, human right activists, environmentalists, women movements and other people's movements are spear-heading the campaign for a perfect society or social order. The movements of civil society and Anna Hazare, the Narmada Bachao Andolan (Medha Patkar) and the human right activities of Swami Agnivesh are the examples for this. Our understanding of perfection cannot be perfect, unless our faith is socially committed or praxis-oriented to have a perfect Christian life and mission.

CHAPTER VIII

SYNCRETISM AND THE ISRAELITES

The modern age is an era of confusion. There is confusion of ideas and ideals and even the confusion of beliefs. This perplexities are found in belief, worship, values and practices. This is seen in Hinduism, Buddhism, Islam, Christianity and in almost all religions of the world. The concepts, worship, values and practices of a religion are mixed with another and it takes a new form, which is known as syncretism. Din-e-Ilahi, the religion founded by Akbar the Great was eclectic. The Buddhism of Japan and Thailand took a new shape in the new culture. The Islam also mingled with other cultures and the original form was lost. The examples for it can be traced from Indian context. The Christianity, uncritically, accommodated some non-Christian elements from other cultures. I would, in this attempt, like to analyse the syncretic elements in the belief, worship, ethics and practices of the Israelites.

God has commanded the Israelites to believe and worship Him alone. He revealed Himself to Abraham and called him out to serve His purpose (Gen. 12:1f: Acts 7:2). He has again disclosed Himself and His name to Moses (Ex. 3:2, 14). Moses asked the people to acknowledge Yahweh as the only true God (Deut. 4:35, 39; 6:4). But the people were henotheistic, that is, belief in one God without asserting that he is the only God. Yahweh admonished them that "you shall have no other gods before me" (Deut. 5:7). He expected an unswerving faith from them. The prophets also affirmed the monotheistic belief (Isai. 46:9, Jer. 10:10).

God required from His people the worship. He did not like anybody or anything to be worshipped than Himself. He was deadly against idolatry and worshipping alien gods. Jacob was asking his household to get rid of the gods of Paddan Aram (Gen. 35:2). This indicated that Jacob was aware of the fact that God does not like anything less than the single-eyed devotion and undivided loyalty. The idolatry is nothing else than comparing God with man, animal or any other object. Hence it was strictly forbidden (Ex. 20:21-23; Deut. 4:15 ff; 5:8.9). It was so pathetic that the Israelites violated the sovereign rule and worshipped a golden calf (Ex. 32:2-6). This was a demonstration of the disbelief of the people in Yahweh. This proved that they were not convinced of the reality, majesty and sovereignty of Yahweh. Joshua strongly negated the neutrality in belief and worship (Josh. 24:14,15).

The Israelites worshipped the gods of the peoples around them and disobeyed God. They worshipped Baal and Ashtaroth, the gods and godesses of the cananites and other neighbouring nations (Judg. 2:11-14,17). They distrusted God and were inconsistent in their faith (1 King. 18:21). But Elijah challenged the gods of the nations and proved that Yahweh was the only true God (1 King. 18:37-39). Jehu tried to abolish the Real worship in Israel (II King. 10:25-28). The calf worship was continued in the northern kingdom (I King 12:26 ff). The Israelites did even worship the idols which are brought from Egypt (Ezk. 20:7.8). The Baal worship was increasingly continued in Judah (Jer. 11:13). They also burned incense before Baal. They secretly worshipped the 'queen of heaven' and other deities, while they publicly confessed Yahweh as the 'only true God'. Their private and public convictions and confessions were diametrically opposite (Jer. 44:18-19). Yahweh ridiculed the 'god' of Babylon (Isai 46:6; 44:9-18). The futility of idolatry had also been affirmed by prophet Jeremiah. He portrayed the idol as a scarecrow. Their gods are, in his words, deaf and dumb (Jere. 10:5).

Worshipping objects, human beings and mamon are the idolatry and it can be equated to the belief and worship of the Israelites who drifted away from Yahweh. God never tolerates the divided loyalty, since it is an infidelity, disregard, dishonour and distrust. The vested interests, selfish goals and the wrong teachings misguide the people.

The faith and worship are not the end, but only the beginning. God also provided an ethics to this people. The faith should be exercised and it must be reflected in thoughts and deeds. God never forbear the immorality and injustice. The people of Sodom and Godmorrah had practiced homosexuality, but God punished them severely (Gen. 19:5). Joseph had got a opportunity to fulfil his carnal desires, but the values he held did not allow him to yield (Gen. 39:8-12). The Decalogue also instructed to honour parents and to restrain from murder, adultery, false testimony and covetousness (Ex. 20).

The cultic prostitution was found in Palestine in connection with worship of Baal and Ashtaroth (1 King. 14:24, 15:12; 1 Sam. 2:2; II King 23:7). The Israelites also involved in shameful and ignoble sexual immorality such as adultery, incest and prostitution (Amos 2:7,

Ezk. 22:11; Hosea 4:10; Jer. 5:7.8). The law of God was utterly violated by the israelites (Lev. 19:29; Deut. 23:18). They went after the momentary pleasures as they engaged in extra-marital and pre-marital sexual immoralities. The transitory pleasures tend them to break the eternal rule of God. The inordinate sexual passion blinded their eyes, and involved even in incest.

God reminds them also of the social responsibility (Ex. 22:16-23:9; Lev. 25). God hates the favouritism, oppression, exploitation and injustice. He wants everybody to assist one another inorder to have an egalitarian society. The Bible also gives equal importance to vertical and horizontal relationships. God does not like His people to go unbridled. The restrictions are to lead the people on the proper path. God is just and righteous (Ps. 71:2; 72:1,2). The importance of justice is stressed by the prophets (Amos 5:15, 24, Mic. 6:8). God wants everybody to be straight and right in their attitudes, thoughts, deeds and dealings. God has admonished the people, since they suppressed the poor and lived in luxury at the expense of the poor (Hos 12:7; Amos 2:6,7a).

The practices are another significant aspect to be discussed. God never allowed the Israelites to follow whatever they like. God has repudiated the divination, soothsaying, enchantments, sorcery, human sacrifice, mediums, necromancy, witchcraft, and interpreting omens (Lev. 19:26; Dt. 18:9-14; II King, 17:17; 21:6). Consulting the mediums and using divinations are reflecting the disbelief in God. In order to get guidance in some personal and social matters, they are supposed to look to God. When the Philistines encamped against King Saul, he had gone upto the witch of Endor to know what would be the consequence of the battle (I Sam. 27:8ff). These practices are detestable and disobedience to our God since these are from the power of darkness.

It is quite essential to examine ourselves in the light of these Old Testament observations. Everyone should evaluate their belief, worship, ethics and practices so that it will enable to discern the syncretic elements and to undergo a reformation. The principles put forward by God is relevant and applicable to all times. God hates the formalism and nominalism. He only looks for the whole hearted commitment to Him (Dt. 6:5). He expects from everyone the absolute dependence, unchanging loyalty, unshakeable faith and an unswerving morality.

CHAPTER IX

LIFE IN FULLNESS IS THE RIGHT OF EVERYONE

Fullness in life is what humanity is seeking for. Jesus said that He came to give life and life in abundance or in fulness (John 10:10). Life in fullness includes the welfare, well being and wholeness of the whole of creation. Everyone has the right to enjoy the life in fullness. For christianity, even the death is a celebration of life, as there is hope of a glorious life or life in fullness beyond death.

The concept of 'life' or 'life in fullness is central to Jesus' teaching. The theology of life is very found in an elaborate sense in the Gospel of John. Jesus is portrayed as the vivifier, one who gives life. Jesus is the source of life and giver of life. Jesus said 'I am the life and resurrection', 'I am the bread of life' and 'those who believe in me has life' (John. 11). Logos (Christ) is explained as the light of life (John 1). The cross and resurrection provide clue for the concept of life in fullness. The incarnation of Jesus is to give life to humanity. The vicarious suffering of Jesus on the cross is for the life fullness of the humanity and for the whole of creation. Resurrection of Jesus was a challenge to the structures of death and evil which against fullness of life. Jesus did sacrifice his own life for the life-in-fullness of others.

The concept of life in fullness is a dynamic process of humanization. It is liberative. In the context of oppression and victimization life-affirmation is significant. It is redeeming and liberating. Poverty, indignity, marginalization, corruption, exploitation of resources, pollutions and criminality have become the main symbols of the day, which are the symbols of death. But some sectors have misunderstood them as life or portrayed them as life. The mafias are good and keen on presenting the symbols of death as life. There is no life in fullness, where there is no justice.

The dalits, tribes, fishfolk, victimized women, slum-dwellers, the poor and other marginalized groups are looking for life in fullness or a fuller humanity. Here the question of ethics of survival or politics of survival is very crucial. Everyone has the right to have dignified life. The fair distribution of resources, fairness in opportunities and participation in the decision-making only will help facilitate life in fullness. As fullness in life is the hope and aim of everyone, the identity, dignity and rights of everyone have to be safeguarded.

The meeting of World Council of Churches was held in Busan, South Korea in the year 2013. The theme chosen for the conference is 'God of life — lead us to peace and justice'. The Kingdom of God is central to this theme as peace and justice play vital role in it. It is also quite ecological. God is the source of life. Life symbolizes green, and God is green. Water, air, land and other resources are basic for life, and without these no one can survive. Protecting the life, even wild life, bio-diversity and resources like water, fuel and minerals are important for the meaningful survival of the universe. Preserving the resources is a concept of eco-justice. The use of pesticides like endosulfan is violence against eco-system.

The sanctity of life is also another important issue. '*Ahimsa*' (Non-violence) and *Aparigraha* (non-possession) are very significant Indian concepts which stand for sanctity of life and preservation. These concepts are non-egoistic and pro-life. Irresponsible abortions, foeticide, and brutal killing including the 'honour killing' are a challenge to life in fullness. There are issues like 'missing women' in the world because of female foeticide. Life has to be protected, but no life is safe even in the womb of the mother. Life can be destroyed even before the birth. Irresponsible abortions and active euthanasia are manipulations on life and they are to be condemned.

The war, terrorism, fundamentalism and ethnic crises also contribute to death. They are hindrances to life in fullness. They are the symbols of death-in-fullness. The dropping of Atom bombs 'the little boy' and 'fat man' (the names given to Atom bombs) in Hiroshima and Nagasaki (Japan) have killed at the moment itself (August 6 and 9, 1945) around 1,75,000 people. Millions are suffering from Atomic Radiation syndrome. The life of people are in a threatening situation as people are to run away for life as they loose their property, relatives and their own family members. The peace, justice and security are essential for life in fulness.

Another major issue today is the misuse of electronic media. The cyber space is irresponsibly used. The misuse of internet, mobile phones, computer discs, pen drives have become the symbols of death. They can be used responsibly, but these are misused which leads to caricature of personalities, deceptions, sex traps, suicides and murder. We live in a world of temptation, consumerism and deception where the inclination to death is increasing and the move towards life is declining.

Life in fullness is for harmony, co-existence, pro-existence and humanization. The meaningful survival on this universe by all beings is very essential. We have to overcome the discriminations in the name of caste, class, race and gender in order to affirm life in fullness. The right to live in dignity and the right to have life in fullness is to be emphasized in every sphere of life.

SECTION B

REFLECTIONS ON BIBLICAL ISSUES

CHAPTER X

THE PROPHETS AND THE CULT

The prophets stood for correcting the evil practices. The prophets rejected the ways in which the offering is made before God. The sacrifices and rituals became peripheral and lost their inner meaning. The prophets ask them "wash yourselves; make yourselves clean: remove the evil of your doings." The people forget many things such as correcting oppressive ways, and pleading for widows, but where giving undue importance to sacrifice and festivals. God looks for obedience, justice and goodness than sacrifice and cultic worship. More than burnt offerings, obedience is emphasized. Sacrifice is an expression of a living faith in the Lord may be a genuine religious act, but Lord's delight is in the true knowledge of the demands of his service and the cultivation of love.

The prophets were given more importance to inner life and its reflection in social life of a person than the sacrifice and rituals. Amos says, when injustice prevails, assemblies, sacrifice and rituals are not meaningful. The trangressions and evil increased in this situation, so clean and wash ourselves and come to the Lord to offer sacrifices.

The prophets were, of course, not against the priestly religion. Many references in the Bible says that prophets and priests worked together. Some scholars say that some prophets are cultic officers. They lived in the sanctuaries as officers as priests. They involved in sacrifice, festival and all other cultic practices. According to R.E. Clements, the prophets did not oppose all cults as such, in favour of a non-cultic religion, but they opposed the cult which they found because it no longer expressed the ethical nature of true Yahwism (refer R.E. Clements, *Prophecy and Covenant*).

Lindblom in his book '*Prophecy in Ancient Israel*' says it was a special class of 'cultic prophets', in strict sense, prophets who were more firmly attached to the sanctuaries as members of the ordinary cultic staff, who received maintenance from the sanctuary, like priests and cultic functionaries. Priests and prophets are often mentioned in the intimate connection with each other. In the activity of the prophets there is much that is akin to the world of cultic ideas and practices. Attention has been drawn in recent years to the probability that there were cultic prophets attached to the shrines alongside with priests and that so far from prophet and priest being exponents of opposed types of religion, they long flourished side by side as fellow officials of the cultus. There is another view that since prophets were religious persons, devotees of their God, it is natural to find them in the shrines in which religion centred. But that does not mean that they are the members of the shrines.

Anyway the prophets were not against cultic practices. They so negatively spoke against it because the priests and people became corrupt. The justice is gone, obedience and truth are vanished. People argued for sacrifices as there was trangressions and evil and they did not clean themselves. The prophets so negatively spoke because of the lack of inner change. They were also not against priestly religion. The prophets reminded them to practice it with keeping the rules and regulations. Mostly prophets were not in sanctuaries, they stood between the people and preached against in the corruption of priests in the sanctuary. According to R.E. Clements, the cult becomes divorced from righteousness and obedience to Yahweh.

Following is a reflection on the Relevance of this OT prophetic-priestly conflict to the life and worship of todays Christian church in India.

Of course, there is a conflict or misunderstanding in the church between the religious authorities and others because they say that the church is not functioning properly. The church lost its vision to mission, and church is to be renewed, based on Biblical foundations. In the Indian context the prophets are not other than people with great vision and those who believe and know the biblical truth.

The 'priestly-prophetic' conflict of OT is very relevant today in the Indian churches. People are even leaving the churches because of its strong traditionalism and non-biblical practices. They stand inside and outside the church and strongly argue for a renewal.

The worship in the churches becomes so traditional and only pre-occupied on the rituals. The life style of a christian priest is lost and church and priests became the corrupted ones. They lost the vision of mission. They became selfish. Two kinds of prophets were seen in the Indian context. Some are leaving the traditional church and stand outside and try to correct the church. Some are standing inside and correct the church. They participate in all activities of the church. They are in the life of the church but criticized many evil practices.

In the Christian churches of India, there are lot of confusion about the worship. Some members are fed up with the existing worship patterns. They say that it becomes a routine and no one is benefited from worship to build up the inner life and social concern. Many people say the church worship should be renewed and revived. Another may say the church worship becomes unbiblical, there are elements to be renewed. There are groups who may say the church has not the only the responsibility to worship, but it should lead members to witness. The failure of the church is also leading to the reason for the formation of para-church organizations.

BIBLIOGRAPHY

Lindblom, J., *Prophecy in Ancient Israel*, Oxford: Basil Blackwell, 1962.
Young, E.J., *My Servant the Prophets*, Michigan: Wim Eerdmans Publisher, 1974.
Rowley, H.H., *The Servant of the Lord and Other Essays on the OT*, London: Lutherworth Press, 1952.
Clements, R.E., *Prophecy and Covenant*, Oregon: Wipf and Stock Publishers, 2009.
Gerhard, Von, *OT Theology*, Vols. I & II, Edinburg: Oliver & Boyd, 1962, 65.
R.K. Harrison, *OT Introduction*, Leicester: IVP, 1970.

CHAPTER XI

THE PROPHETS AND SOCIAL JUSTICE

It was the goal of the wealthy to make the poor, more poor (Amos 8:4-6) so that they would be forced to sell themselves into slavery. The wealthy were interested in exploiting the poor, and the authorities were in league with them. They had the mania of acquring the land and houses, this was acquired by violence and exploitation. The rulers ignore the fact that they were entrusted with the righteousness and justice. In Amos 6:1-6, we see that the merchants used false measures and decided against the poor and killed prophets. The bribery was promoted everywhere. Pride and self-indulgence, moral bankruptcy and callousness prevailed everywhere (Isaiah 5:8-23). There was a shocking contrast between extreme rich and extreme poverty. The worship became syncretic. Joh Bright says that Amos' message was a devastating attack on the social evils of the day, particularly on the heartlessness and dishonesty with which the rich had ground upon the poor (2:6f, 5:10-12, 8:4-6), but also on the immorality and the careless pursuit of luxury which had badly affected the national character (2:7, 4:1-3, 6:1-6) all of which he viewed as sins that Yahweh would surely punish. The rich ones oppressed the peasants and farmers too.

We can see a lot of parallels in the Indian Socio-economic scene too. In India the trade and other income-generating areas are on the hands of the rich, and land is also in the hands of these rich people. There are corruption and bribery in Government administrative bodies. On the one side, people are enjoying in the ivory tower and had luxurious life, but on the other side poverty, begging, no shelter, no food and no one to care. In the government offices the poor are neglected to get rights. The bribery and corruption are prevailing everywhere. If poor people wants something to be done, they have to give bribe or gifts to the officials otherwise he has to suffer much. Even Judges in the courts are influenced by bribes. So that the rich can give more bribes and get advantage over the poor. The authorities are doing everything on the basis of how much bribe we have paid to them. The false measures are used by the merchants to cheat the poor. The land owners are exploiting the poor farmers and peasants. They are paid low wages and trade and commerce were monopolized by them. The rich are getting much profit without much effort. The false measures are common among the traders and merchants. They mostly cheat the illiterates and aboriginals (Adivasis) with these measures.

In the society the caste system, racism, and class system are playing dominant roles. The society is divided into many compartments. The high caste people looked down on the low caste and neglect them. In some areas they were used by the so called high caste people as slaves. The moral life of the people is degenerating. The prostitution, adultery, rape, and other moral evils are prevailing in the city and village.

There are many bases and motives behind the prophets' venture to stand against injustice and oppression. The prophets were responsible for protecting and restoring the right. Righteousness is the essence of worship. The justice and righteousness should be maintained in society and in the temple then only worship is pleasing to God.

In Isaiah 58, prophet was very directly telling them not to oppress poor and do only justice so that God may please in worship and fasting. In the scripture, the people of God are commanded to execute justice. God is the one who vindicates the oppressed and defends the weak (Ps. 103:6). When justice is properly executed, the people are the agents or the instruments of the divine will (Isa. 59:15-16). God is the lover of Justice and he hates evil and oppession and corruption. Israel's cult became a place of sin as there was immorality and social evils so the prophets have reminded the Israelites of their covenant relationship and the nature of God they are serving and worshipping. The prophets are entrusted with the message of God to correct and lead them in the right path. They wanted to keep the society and religious life and to be obedient towards God's will and purpose. They worked for a just society where there is no domination, corruption, injustice but the overflowing of the righteousness of God.

The Indian church has a greater responsibility to do much on these respects. India is a country where there is much oppression and injustice. There are many people who are suffering from different needs. The church in India is a prophet to curb the oppression of the powerful over the poor. But in order to do that, the Indian church should think of herself. If these injustices such as prejudice, racism, caste system, domination and tug of war for position are prevailing in it, how can the church be a public witness. If the christian businessmen, landowners, and officers of the government service are agents of exploitation, corruption, bribery and fake measures the purging of the church is the first concern. The church many a times forget the responsibility.

The church should have a prophetic role within and also in the society. India is badly in need of educational and medical institutions to serve the poor. On the other side the farmers and the poor are in need of getting justice from government and other offices. Certainly church can do many things in this respect. church is the 'light' to lead the society and government in the right path but the church is neglecting the needs of the society. She is content with the worship and other services, and neglect the moral responsibility towards society.

The Indian society is morally degraded. But the preachers or christian ministers are not emphasizing the sin in their preaching. They even neglect the Biblical teaching of evil. The social issues are to be discussed by the church. The christian ministers should preach about the necessity of a just society. According to sider "Neglect of the Biblical teaching on structural injustices and institutionalized evil is one of the omissions in evangelicalism today" (Rich christians in the *Age of Hunger*, by Ronald J. Sider).

The main concern of the church should be society, a just society devoid of evil and moral degeneration. As mentioned earlier the church must be light and it should act as a prophet in the society. Justice is to be found in the church and society. According to Mott, Justice is a duty to bring all who are economically disadvantaged to the point where they have the capacity to participate in the full life of the community (Dt. 15.4). The orphan and the widow are the examples of oppression's victims.

BIBLIOGRAPHY

Bright, John, *A History of Israel*, London: SCM Press, 1982.

Samuel, Vinay and Sugden, Chris, "Social Justice: Biblical and Practical", *Traci Journal*.

Mott, Stephen C., *Biblical Ethics and Social Change*, New York: Oxford University Press, 1982.

Sider, Ronald, *Rich christians in the Age of Hunger*, New York: Hodder & Stoughton, 1973.

CHAPTER XII

THE EXISTENCE AND CHARACTER OF THE NATION OF ISRAEL AND ITS RELEVANCE TO THE NATURE AND MISSION OF THE CHRISTIAN CHURCH

Introduction

The existence and the character of Israel as a nation is very significant. They were chosen as a model community and their influence to the world in relation to life and ethics have very much contributed to the theology and the framework of the early church and the nature of mission.

A. ***The Existence of Israel as a Nation and Its Distinctives***

Israel was much related to the call of Abraham. A covenant and promise was made by God with Abraham. These are the important promises 'I will make of you a great nation', 'I will bless you', 'by you all the families of the earth shall blessed' (Gen-12: 1ff). They were called to bless all other nations though they were against God and His purpose. This promise reflects the whole purpose and nature of Israel in relation to the other nations. For God's purpose was not meant only for righteous individuals, but for the formation of a new community, by which in their social life would embody those qualities such as righteousness, peace, justice and love. The Israelites believed in the uniqueness of their historical origin. The exodus, covenant in Sinai, and gift of land are the important factors (Dt. 4:32-34).

They were called as a separate and holy people to God, but they went to Egypt and suffered. But God did not forsake them, instead God intervened and saved them miraculously from the bondage of Egypt. God is always concerned with the political and spiritual deliverance of the people. These are important religious distinctiveness to this people. They worship one God. They were against the other gods and idols, and stood for Yahweh (Ex. 23:24). There are so many other gods around, but they were commanded to worship Yahweh, the true God who called them and saved them (Dt. 6:14; 7:5; 29:16-19). As a distinctive people of God they worshipped and served the God Yahweh.

The ethical distinctives of the people are reflecting the character of God, as a witness to the neighbouring nations while other nations are practicing adultery, idolatry, oppression and exploitation. The people of God were called for a new dimension of life and ethics or morality (1 kg 18:20-46, Isa 1:13-17 cf Isa. 58; Mic. 3). The people of Israel had to lead a life which is pleasing to God, i.e. which reflects the concern and character of God. It is in order be a witness to other neighbouring nations. The other nations must come to a relation with God, and Israel as nation must work as a "leaven" or "light".

The covenantal relationship with Israel was another significant factor. This is a very important factor in relation to Israel as a significant people to God. Yahweh is found by Israel as king (Dt. 4:15-16 cf Ex. 20: 4-6). At Sinai, Israel entered into relationship with the invisible King enthroned, "I will be your God, and you shall be my people." The covenant at Sinai required decision. Israel was called to choose or reject. The covenant also points to the future, "I will be your God, and you shall be my people". Israel's commitment to the covenant was voluntary. In her life the covenant was completely oriented to God's sovereignty and Grace. The ethical terminology of the Old Testament is derived from the covenant relationship. "Righteousness" (sedeqah) steadfast love ('Hesed') are covenantal words. Then comes Justice (mispat) and peace (shalom) (Hosea 2:19-20 and Jeremiah 22:16). The marriage terminology is used in the Old Testament in order to make known the relationship between Israel and God. The "faithfulness" was asked by God from the people of Israel. But many times the people neglected and ignored these relationships and God has reminded them of this during different times.

A law was given to the people to follow which is quite distinctive for Israel as God's people. The law played a dominant role to distinguish the life style of Israel from others. The election of Israel and its responsibility is another important factor. It is one of the central realities of the Old Testament. Every intervention by God in history is an election; either when he chooses a place in which to make more special manifestation of his presence, or when he chooses a people to carry out his intentions, or when he chooses a man to be his representative or his messenger. When God chooses a man or people or community, it is the responsibility to carry out the message of the one who called (Jere 2:1-7, 3:11-22; Isa 50:11). Yahweh is understood as possession of the people (Ex. 4:22; Isa 63:16; 64:7). The person of Moses played a dominant role in the forming of the elected people, it is the reality of forming of the elected people, it is the reality which cements the unity and faith of the people. Separation implies the demand of belonging to Yahweh and serving him (Am 3:2; Dt. 4:19).

The gift of the land played a crucial role in the life of the people. God has promised of the land which was attained after a long and consistent conflict with many nations. The whole aim of Israel was pointed to the land and that gift was an important factor in their whole life and existence.

The Mission of Israel is very crucial because God has called them to be a witness in the world or the nations around them. Israel was a "priestly community" (Lev 21-22; Ex. 19:5). It has a role of the teacher (Dt. 33:10; Hos 4:6; Malachi 2:4-7). Holiness of Israel was not merely a spiritual but a practical one. The national and social life which must reflect justice, love, compassion, that they would function as God's holy priesthood, as a nation, among the nation, for the nations (Ps. 99:1-4). Israel has failed in the mission that God has entrusted so the prophets criticized and urged them to accomplish.

The suffering servant and His mission is important in this respect. The servant passages are found in the book of Isaiah (Isa 42:18-21; 44:1-5; 50:4-11; 52:13-53:12). Servant is described as one of bringing the light of the knowledge of God and a covenant relationship with him to nation beyond the borders of Israel himself. These passages are very relevant to mission. The fact that Jesus applies these passages to himself show that he regarded himself as assuming his servant role that Israel had failed to fullfill. The purpose of incarnation was to reveal God. The Israelite's existence and character were to be a witness to God, model or paradigm of His holiness expressed in the social life of a redeemed community. The church is related to people of God, and the covenant is related and fullfilled in Christ Jesus. The Gospel was to the gentiles also as Israel was called 'a light to the nations' (Isa. 42:6).

B. *The Significance of Israel in OT Theology*

Israel and Old Testament are very much related. If there is no Israel then there is also no Old Testament Theology. It is not an exaggeration or overreaction. The whole Old Testament Theology is intertwined with God's dealing with Israel. God has revealed Himself to Israel through his words and actions. These people were chosen to become a model of God's intentions in relation to faith, ethics and God's purpose and design to all other nations. The plan of God in relation to the election of gentiles was revealed by God through the prophets. The covenant and election are the significant themes in the OT Theology. The Messiah must come from the chosen people. All God's dealing with the people of Israel is very much involved in the theology of the old testament. The law was given to Israel and it is quite distinctive in the Israel's life and OT Theology. The ethics, worship and relationship with God as people of God, the Israel played a vital role in OT Theology. Israel as a community of God is crucial in OT Theology.

C. *Israel and the "New Israel" in Relation to Mission*

The new Israel and the Israel were very much related. We cannot separate them, though we consider them as separate entities. The covenant with Abraham is fulfilled as Jesus has come as saviour to Abraham's "descendents" (Gal. 3:16, 4:4; Rom 9:4; 9:6-7). The promise of Abraham and gentile mission is very crucial at this point. We can see this in Acts of Apostles (3:25-26) "to bless you in turning everyone of you from your wickedness" and Ephasians (2:12,19) "strangers to the covenant of promise" became "members of the household of God".

The true offspring of Abraham are those who reproduce Abraham's faith, whether they are gentile or Jews (Gen. 22:1 ff; Rom 4:13-16, Heb 6:13-18). The righteousness of faith is the significant factor to become God's people rather than claiming that they were chosen by God as Israel did claim. The New Israel was chosen by God to have a special purpose which Israel could not accomplish, that is "declare the glory of God" (1 Peter 2:9). The new Israel has kept the priesthood and acted as a priest among others to bring others to Christ irrespective of the caste, race, economical and social barriers.

Apostle Paul, the great missionary had preached the message to the gentiles and many churches were planted among the people. The church was open to accept jews and gentiles because the New Israel or church was founded by Christ who has broken the existing barriers between the Jews and gentiles. The church in Corinth, Antioch, Philippi and churches in Galatia and Ephesus were either gentile or mixture of both gentiles and Jews.

The Gentile mission was found in the Old Testament and the privileges were given but people of Israel have enjoyed the privilege and failed to work out the responsibilities they have for others. The Church has taken the responsibility to fulfil the commands given to Israel. So the Church acted as a "light to the nations" in the real sense.

The coming of Messiah in the OT which is fulfilled by coming of Jesus Christ and His mission is very much related. Messiah came as a liberator. Messiah came as a suffering servant to suffer for others.

Conclusion

The existence and character of the nation Israel as God's people certainly influenced a lot and contributed much to the Christian church today as the people of God.

The mission is always God's mission, which was entrusted with Israel in the OT period, and it was done by the New Israel in the NT period. It is so happened that people of Israel had failed in doing God's mission.

BIBLIOGRAPHY

Jacob, E., *Theology of the Old Testament*, New York: Harper & Row, 1955.

Muilenburg, James, *Way of Israel: Biblical Faith and Ethics*, New York: Harper Collins Publishers, 1983.

Bruce, F.F., *This is that, Carlisle*, Paternoster Press, 1968.

Wright, Christopher J.H., *Living as People of God*, London: IVP, 1983.

CHAPTER XIII

THE VISION OF JUBILEE: A PARADIGM FOR STRUCTURAL CHANGE AND LIBERATION

Introduction

This chapter is an attempt to understand the vision of Jubilee from a Liberative Perspective. The vision of Jubilee in the OT, its reflection in the NT, the selected aspects of Jubilee in the history and the implication to present context are the main focus of the presentation.

It should be kept in mind that though the Jubilee was not practiced in its fullness, it must have practiced in some form in the community. It, at least, gave a impetus to live as a community with the spirit of socialism, leaving the spirit of capitalism. Even the concepts like justice, shalom or covenant were not practiced in complete form in Israelite community.

A. *The Vision of Jubilee in OT*

I would like to make some theological and ethical reflections on jubilee. Jubilee challenges the capitalistic ideas that dehumanize people. The vision of Jubilee was given in a feudalistic society to have a prophetic role to challenge capitalism. There was accumulation of wealth in the Israelite society as many become landless. Slavery was practiced. The poor were exploited and oppressed. They were disempowered, as power was concentrated by the powerful.

The vision of Jubilee (Lev. 25) has portrayal of the reality of the time and it provides measures for restoration. It was not a charity and sharing of resource but returning the income generating resource to the original owners who are now powerless and poor. The slaves are to be free. No one should be in bondage. The liberation or emancipation of the marginated is the essence of biblical message. In Exodus and Deuteronomy (Exodus 23:9; 21:2-21; Dt. 15:15), we have the instructions that do justice to slaves, aliens and poor and do not oppress them. According to Christopher J.H. Wright, "In Leviticus (25:35-55) there are regulations concerning various degrees of impoverishment and the steps to be taken by the better off kinsman. No less than three times the latter is reminded of the exodus as motivation for fair treatment of the poorer brother (vv. 38, 42, 55; cf. 26:13)." (*Living as the People of God*, Leicester: IVP, 1983, p. 29).

The OT has the motive clauses (Dt 15:5) which is to persuade the people to obey (*Ibid.*, p. 30). The vision is given to be obeyed so that there would be transformation in attitude, relationships and perspectives. Considering the 'other' is important as aliens, slaves and poor are to be accepted as people with identity, dignity and rights. The social structure was so evil that the marginated are in a dehumanized situation. Their restoration is a distant dream. The corrupt society was exploiting and oppressing so much, so that they are pushed to the extreme corner. This is found in the form of slavery and in shelterless, landless conditions. Jubilee is a year of joy, happiness, restoration and liberation from the clutches of unfreedom and bondage. It is the trumpet of triumph for the poor and powerless.

The jubilee is a completion of seven seven-year cycle. It is the fiftieth year. According to R.K Harrison, "The conservation of natural and other resources which is prescribed by this legislation forms the basis of good agricultural and ecological practice" (Leviticus: *An Introduction and Commentary*, Leicester: IVP, 1980, p. 223). He continued to state, "The Jubilee legislation had as its basic theme the liberation of that which was bound. As a result it reminded the Israelites every fifty years of the fact that once the people of God had been bound in Egypt, victims of an oppressive native regime, but that they had been liberated at the exodus by a miraculous display of divine power" (*Ibid.*, p. 223). The covenant values are asserted in Jubilee. According to Harrison, the legislation provides liberty to those who were in servitude, so it is a restoration. Those who had to dispose their ancestral holdings because of economic problems were able to repossess them. The people were also required to have simple life in the time of Jubilee. God affirms that land and resources are God's (*Ibid.*, p. 223).

Discussing the issues of Jubilee, Walter Brueggemann observes that the land itself have the periodic rest from cultivation which may help the land not to be exhausted from overuse. It also indicates that land belongs to God. In his opinion, Yahweh is the God who enacted the Exodus (Lev. 25:38, 42, 55) proposes social practices designated to perpetuate the Exodus community. He argues that it is difficult to imagine a more radical social possibility that the Sabbatic principle, particularly as it leads to the Jubilee year (*Theology of the Old Testament*, Minneapolis: Fortress Press, 1997).

Jubilee has a vision of radical restructuring of socio-economic structures. It is a dynamic exercise which is liberative. The dynamism and liberation are playing vital role here. Don't misinterpret it as imaginary and unrealistic. The word 'utopia' is misused to interpret any vision as unrealistic. The British novelist Thomas Moore has the novel named '*Utopia*' is based on a socialistic vision where there is a affirmation of equitable distribution of resources, the dignity and rights of powerless and the eight hours of work for proletariat. These are all realized in history in one form or other. Reducing the power of socialistic vision as utopia is to reduce the dynamic-liberative power of the vision. These reductions and deviations are the agenda of the capital-intensive society.

The prophetic vision is also socialistic. The prophets were trying to transform the society from the clutches of evil such as the exploitation, oppression and corruption. The prophets have integrated the vision of the covenant, Jubilee, law and the messianic kingdom (millennial rule). The integral liberation is promised in book of Isaiah (Isa 61:1ff). They have an eschatological vision of a new world order where there is no injustice and oppression. The age to come is an age of Jubilee for them (Isa 9:2-7). Jubilee is God's plan of restoration and transformation which may be undermined by humanity by their selfish interests.

A radical restoration of land, wealth and dignity is promoted by Jubilee. In Jubilee the slaves, poor and the disempowered are to be rejoiced as there is restoration of land, power and relationship. Jubilee is also has ecological significance as a land also received rest as ethics of care is applied to the creation or nature. The eco-justice plays a very crucial role in the context of Jubilee. Jubilee gives space to have restoration with God, humanity and creation. Jubilee is a great Sabbath. There is concern for poor, aliens and slaves. It also prohibits interest to the loans (Lev 25:38).

B. *The Vision of Jubilee in NT*

Jubilee has very important dimensions in the NT. Jesus was relating Jubilee with Kingdom of God and his ministry. Incarnation itself is a Jubilee of God. It is Jubilee to whole of humanity and creation. Jesus said "come to me, all who labour and are heavy laden, and I will give you rest" (Mt. 11:28). The Gospel itself is the message of Jubilee.

Robert North discusses four things about Jubilee in relation to NT, according to Gordon J. Wenham.

Robert North discusses the lessons a Christian may learn from this chapter under four heads: social justice, social worship, personal values and messianic typology. His discussion is difficult to improve on, and here some of his main points are summarized.

Social Justice

The Jubilee was intended to prevent the accumulation of the wealth of the nation in the hands of a very few. Every Israelite had an inalienable right to his family land and to his freedom. If he lost them through failing into debt he recovered them in the Jubilee. The biblical law is opposed equally to the monopolistic tendencies of unbridled capitalism and thorough-going communism, where all property is in state's hands. By keeping land within a particular family, the Jubilee also promoted family unity.

Social Worship

The Jubilee is presented in this chapter as an extension of the Sabbath day and sabbatical year (vv. 3ff). True religion is not opposed to a just society. Concern for the one should go hand in hand with concern for other. The prophetic words "I desire mercy and not sacrifice" (Hos. 6:6; Matt. 9:13; 12:7) was a word to a society who thought God would be satisfied with sacrifice by itself. Had they paid attention to Leviticus, the men of Hosea's day might not have made that mistake.

Personal Values

"Love your neighbour as yourself" (Lev. 19:18) is the all-embracing moral principle that inspires the Jubilee legislation. The NT too recognizes that the rich have an obligation to give to the poor (e.g., 1 John 3:17; Jas 2:15ff). The Jubilee also draws attention to the fleeting nature of man's earthly abode: *you are resident aliens and settlers with me* (v. 23). Equally Christians recognize that they are but pilgrims and sojourners here and look for another city "whose builder and maker is God" (Heb 11:10). Finally, believers in both covenants are assured that those who put God's will first will have all their physical needs provided (Lev. 25:18ff.; cf Matt. 6:25ff).

Messianic Typology

At Nazareth Jesus Declared (Luke 4:18-19):

> *"he has sent me to proclaim release to the captives and recovering of sight to blind, to set at liberty those who are oppressed, to proclaim the acceptable year of the lord."*

In Isa. 61.1, from which Jesus was quoting, the word used for "release" (deror) is the same as that found in Lev. 25:10. It seems quite likely, therefore, that the prophetic description of the "acceptable year of the lord" was partly inspired by the idea of the Jubilee year. The messianic age brings liberty to the oppressed and release to the captives.

This age was inaugurated with Christ's first coming (Luke 4:21). It will be completed by his second coming (Jas. 5:1-8; cf. Luke 16:19-31). The Jubilee, then, not only looks back to God's first redemption of his people from Egypt (Lev. 25:38, 55), but forward to the "restitution of all things," "for new heavens and a new earth in which righteousness dwells" (Acts 3:21; 2 Pet. 3:13). (Gordon J. Wenham, *The Book of Leviticus* (NICOT), Michigan: Wm. Eerdmans Publishing Co., 1979, pp. 323-24).

The Nazareth manifesto provides (Lk 4:16-21) the clue that the kingdom of God is ushered in and the messianic rule has begun. There is offer of Good news to the poor and liberation for the subaltern people who are oppressed. There is hope for integral liberation for the specially abled (or People with Disabilities) and the downtrodden. The poor masses are empowered and liberated through the incarnation of the divine in the form of Jesus Christ.

There is Jubilee as justice, love and peace to the marginated, though the rich and powerful became restless. The Kingdom of God foresees a community of Love, Peace and Justice. Jesus' mission was to emancipate the poor and powerless from the clutches of unfreedom. The spiritual, physical and psychological bondage was the reality in Jesus time and Jesus had liberated the people from that bondages. Many were slaves to demonic power who were set free by Jesus. The unjust socio-economic structure had made many poor and kept marginated. Jesus had challenged the unjust structure and liberated them.

Jesus challenged the dehumanizing powers as humanization was the agenda of Jesus' mission. The affirmation of God's justice, equitable distribution of resources and the liberation of subaltern are the key elements in Jesus' mission. He asked the rich and the powerful to sell their property and distribute to the poor. He ridiculed those who accumulated wealth for their selfish well being. Being understood the message of Jesus Christ, Zachaeus is willing to return the money that was collected by unjust manner. By challenging the rich and powerful, Jesus was attacking the exploitative structure of the time.

The subalterns occupy a central place in Jesus' perspective as they are the victims of evil social structure. A sociological and political reading of the New Testament is important to understand the undercurrents of the time that victimized the powerless. The contrapuntal reading of post-colonialism and the reconstructions of post-modernism and the subversive reading have very crucial roles to play in understanding the implications of Jubilee in the New Testament.

The texts are to be read from the context of the people with varieties of experiences and also from the context of the other. The alternative reading is important as we have to understand the texts and the concepts in the light of questions of the people from the grassroots. All theology and interpretations are to be political and people-oriented rather than elitistic, peripheral or superfluous. It should bring structural change and radical transformation or liberation. We should not be subsumed by otherworldly thinking and the peripheral spirituality.

The dynamic liberative approach in theology and interpretation enable us to interpret the Bible and the concepts in order that the dynamic dimension of liberation will be explored which may be an irruption in theology. This is very much found in the Biblical interpreters and theologians who are consciously and objectively understanding the text in the light of the struggles, aspirations and experiences of the people. Since this is a very creative and reflective paper, quoting scholars is found to be very minimal. Reading the texts from below is very significant as it is subaltern reading.

Jubilee plays a central role in liberation theologians. It is the humanization in M.M. Thomas, it is the andric practice in Sebastian Kappen, it is the love to nature in Samuel Rayan, it is the radical liberation of the marginalized in K.C. Abraham, it is the empowerment and emergence of the blacks, minjung, victimized women, dalits, tribes, transgender and disabled in their concerned theology.

The victimized, the 'other' and the colonized are decolonized and empowered and the subalterns are set free by the Jubilee declaration of the Jesus Christ. This Jubilee is the ushering in of the realized Kingdom of God as C.H. Dodd has indicated. There is peace, justice and empowerment to the subaltern. An objective reading of the New

Testament Gospels will expose the fact that the liberty of the oppressed is the main concern and that is the Jubilee for them. Jesus listened to the cry of the powerless and healed them and liberated them, fed them and preached the good news to them (Jn. 5:1ff; Jn 8:1ff; Jn. 4:1ff; Jn. 6:1ff; Mk. 5:1ff). There is deritulization (Paul Tillich) and dynamic liberation in Jesus understanding of Jubilee as he healed on the Sabbath and cleansed the temple (Mt. 21:12ff).

The influence of the concept of Jubilee plays an important role in the early Christian community as there is a dynamic form of fellowship (koinonia) found (Acts 2:43-47; 4:32-35). The Pentecost and the dynamic appearance of the Holy spirit is a radical liberative aspect of deritualization and reconstruction. It brings joy to people who are in fossilized Jewish religiosity. A strong sense of communitarianism came to be realized in the early Christian community. It asserted the praxiological dimension of the essence of Jubilee (Jas. 2:1-10; 2:14-21). It is very evident that the Jubilee is a time of renewal and rejoicing in hope. The essence of Jubilee is that the resources are to be shared fairly with the poor and powerless. It also has ecological significance as the land also needs rest. The whole creation is also looking forward of transformation (Rom. 8:18-23). The ultimate is to come in the form of the transformation of the whole creation, but the penultimate is found in the form of Jubilee in a wider sense as we try to create a society based on Justice, Equality and Peace.

C. *The Traces of the Jubilee in History*

The Jubilee in the fuller form is not practiced by any community, but there are traces found in several communities. There is equality, justice and shalom prevail in several communities and the ideal of Jubilee is applied by some.

In the Qumran community "Life in the community was of communal nature, including the common meal" (William Sanford Lasor, *The Dead Sea Scrolls and the Christian Faith*, Chicago: Moody Press, 1956, p. 83), in the communal life, the means of producing wealth as well as the wealth itself was to be held in common (*Ibid.*, p.83). They also had a common fund as the regulation in the Damascus document is that the wages of two days in a month were to be put in the hands of supervisor and judge to be used for orphans, the poor and needy, the old man, the prisoner, the maiden without a relative, the virgin with no one to give her in marriage and all the works of the corporation (*Ibid.*, p. 84).

The land and wealth is God's. William Lasor quotes the communality practiced by the Quibbutz in modern Israel. It is so communal that there is no private wealth. Everyone receives according to the need. The wealth is always kept common (*Ibid.*, pp. 85-86). It is assumed that Jubilee vision or a sort of socialistic vision was found in the communitarian life in Qumran.

The church fathers had integrated the message of Jubilee in their life including the sharing of resources to the empowerment of the poor. The second century church father Clement of Alexandria said that luxury is irrational for it mistakes the purpose and end of man. Analysing Clement's thought, Eric Osborn states "Luxury throws all things, out of order. It doesn't observe the course of nature or the proper order of things. Pleasures and luxury brings men to shipwrecks and go against all that is true. The irrational effects of luxury are shown by the neglect of the orphan children" (*Ethical Patterns in Early Christian Thought*, London: Cambridge University Press, 1976, p. 55.).

St. Basil (Basil, born in Caesarea in about A.D. 330) had integrated the message of the Jubilee and the Kingdom of God in his teachings. He had strong vision of an egalitarian society. He stresses the fact that the poor are to be cared. He argued that what is done for the least of his/her brothers or sisters is done to the Lord (*Ibid.*, p. 107). Basil insists that the second pair of shoes and the extra set of clothes is not ours, but of others who are poor.

John Chrysostum was born at Antioch in the middle of fourth century. The socialistic and revolutionary spirit of Jubilee is found in Chrysostum. He lived in poverty and stopped luxury and banquets (*Ibid.*, p. 115). He found that luxury is inconsistent with the spirit of the Gospel. He attacked the extravagance and told that they would be better Christians if they looked after the beggars in the street instead of furnishing their toilets in gold (*Ibid.*, p. 117).

There might be several communities who integrated the concept of Jubilee. They are visible in the Christian and secular world. Jubilee paradigm is found in Pentecostalism. Pentecostalism stands for a structural change as it upholds the values of the Kingdom of God, shalom, Justice and the koinonia or sharing. It argues for the emancipation of the subaltern or powerless. For their social and spiritual liberation, many poor and powerless or victimized have become the active members of Pentecostal movement. They have found identity, dignity and rights as they were the victims of economic injustice, racism and casteism. Pentecostalism in the original form foresees a socialistic society where there is distribution of justice and resources. Equity is also an important Pentecostal concept. Pentecostalism challenges any discrimination and inequality in the name of sex, colour, or status.

The liberation movement is also uphold the values laid by Jubilee. The liberation movements and freedom struggle in the context of colonialism or imperialism worked for the restoration of land, freedom, equality, justice and power. Many nations and communities were disempowered and their resources were exploited and the people were oppressed. This was found in Latin America, African and Asian countries. The people had a mass movements for a structural change. In North America, the blacks had a severe struggle for their political freedom, dignity and rights. There are movements of the poor, women, dalits, tribes, slum-dwellers people with disabilities and transgenders. Their emancipatory aspirations and the liberation from the clutches of landless, shelter less conditions and poverty have found fulfilment to an extent in one form or other is an indication of Jubilee. The colonialism, patriarchy, capitalism or feudalism, the casteism and racism have enslaved the powerless which did shatter through the liberative praxis.

The social movements are the paradigms which stood for justice and rights of the powerless. The land is also a major issue in this regard, so also the issues regarding corruption and injustices. The Narmada Valley Andolan was a great struggle against the human rights violation in relation to the land and habitation. The tribes or indigenous people were forcefully evacuated from their habitat and they lost access to the resources. Jubilee is the Jubilee of the poor, but the Narmada Valley project was meant for the Jubilee of the rich and powerful. The poor masses struggled against the injustice of the government machinery to restore their land and resources.

In Chengara, Pathanamthitta District of Kerala, the landless masses are trying to occupy the land. The government authorities were forced to distribute land to these people. It was a movement of the dalits and poor for the land, shelter and resources. The rights of the dalits to have land is an important issue here. Their Jubilee is nothing but having land for their identity and survival. The dalits, tribes, migrant's and refugees are facing the issue of land all over the world and especially in our country also.

The exclusive nationalism of the fundamentalist forces is a threat to the Jubilee of the poor and powerless. They are creating a distorted paradigm to exclude the minorities, refugees and migrants from the right of citizenship. This is introduced through Citizen Amendment Bill

(CAB) and National Register of Citizens (NRC). The discrimination against the people and their nationality in the name of religion is a great threat in the Indian context. The Indian democracy and secularism are facing serious threat today. Instead of restoring the rights of the powerless, the fundamentalist forces are trying to keep them as captives. It is a dangerous attitude towards the humanity. There is no Jubilee for the minority communities in the emergence of the Hindutva Ideology.

Jubilee was a great inspiration for the people of blacks in North America. The Civil Rights movement was a great challenge for the right to identity, dignity and rights. The Blacks were considered as a slave class and they were exploited, oppressed and dehumanized. The black experience and consciousness play vital role in their efforts for liberation. Martin Luther King Jr. was envisioning a new society or community based on the biblical understanding. The emergence of the blacks to the mainstream as they are restored in dignity and rights was a great vision of black movement. The US minorities have been recognized with their dignity, status and rights.

The African National Congress led by Nelson Mandela had made a historic struggle for the Jubilee or liberation against white regime. The colonial powers had denied their right to land and resources. The blacks had struggled for their freedom and rights. The exploitation and oppression of the whites over the blacks was so serious as blacks were considered as slaves. Their humanity was disregarded. An oppressed community had emerged as liberated from the clutches of dehumanization. Their land is restored. The African people were set free as they were liberated from the clutches of alienation and bondage. The political power is restored and the powerless became empowered to rule the nation.

There are social movements and social Action groups stand for the realization of the concept of Jubilee which is seemed to be 'utopian' for some groups. The social movements of the dalits, tribes, women, transgender, differently abled and other marginalized groups and the green movements are for the restoration of Justice concerns. Restoration of the land or habitat, the resources and the preservation of creation are quite important over here.

Conclusion

The concept of Jubilee is socialistic in nature which affirms the identity, dignity and rights of the people as against alienation and oppression.

Jubilee is based on the principle of co-existence and pro-existence. It is also centred around the humanization. The restoration, politics of survival and the liberative efforts are essential perspectives of the concept of Jubilee. Liberation of the subaltern people or the disempowered people is the key to the concept of Jubilee. It is empowerment and emancipation of the oppressed humanity or the victimized and powerless.

SECTION C

REFLECTIONS ON THEOLOGICAL AND ETHICAL ISSUES

CHAPTER XIV

THE LEGACY OF MARTIN LUTHER KING JR. THE CONTRIBUTION TO THE EMERGENCE OF BLACK COMMUNITY

The contribution of Martin Luther King Jr. as a leader of the Blacks for their emancipation was remarkable. He was willing to even risk his life for the cause of the oppressed ones. He worked for the Justice of the Blacks and martyred for that cause.

The Background

The prejudice against blacks was a common feature in America. In 1937, his father, the clergyman named Reverend Martin Luther King Senior, the Minister of Ebenezer church took him (when he was eight years old) to a shop to buy shoes. It is said that the shop assistant refused to serve them unless they moved to the back of the shop, out of sight of other customers. He said, "we will buy shoes sitting here or we won't buy any shoes at all." As the assistant was found unmoved, father and son marched out of the shop as they are challenging the system (Mary Drewery, *Martin Luther King*, Marshalls, p. 7).

The American slavery was based on the negroes of Africa who were brought to United States. They were sold or forcefully brought as slaves. The blacks were auctioned in the slave market, and the owners had even the right to kill them. The Southern states (like Carolina and Georgia) had supported the slavery and others have even questioned slavery. In order to support the whites against the blacks, the southern states in United States had made laws named 'Jim Crow'. By this law, the blacks were not allowed to enter the restaurants where the whites are present and they were not allowed to sit in the seats of the buses which were reserved for whites. The whites also have organized a movement named 'Ku Klux Klan' to confront the blacks. It was a secret movement which had attacked the blacks in a cruel manner.

Martin Luther King Jr. was an eloquent preacher. He realized that the blacks were considered inferior to the whites. He liked to become a doctor or lawyer, but he became a priest. He started his college education at Morehouse College in Atlanta and continued his theological education in Crozer Seminary in Pennsylvania. He received his doctorate in the year 1955 from Boston University. He married Coretta Scott and had three children. In 1964 he received the Nobel Prize for Peace.

The Philosophy of Martin Luther King

Martin Luther King was a priest, a reformer and revolutionary. He was a freedom fighter of the blacks and a leader of the civil right movement. He followed the paths of non-violence as a follower of Jesus Christ and Mahatma Gandhi.

According to Mary Drewery, "Mahatma Gandhi was the inspiration of much of Martin Luther King's thinking, in particular his non-violent method of protest. At the time, the Martin-led Montgomery bus boycott was likened to Gandhi's famous 'Salt March' to Dandi in 1930" (*Martin Luther King*, p. 41). As Gandhiji was challenging the unjust laws of British Government through civil disobedience, Martin was also using the same means of a boycott in a campaign for civil rights (*Ibid.*, p. 41).

Martin Luther King was referred by Ramin Jahanbegloo (Director of Mahatma Gandhi Centre for Peace, Jindal Global University, Sonipet) as the prophet of non-violence ("The Dream He Had", *The Hindu* (April 3, 2018, p. 9). He continued to state, "As such, his greatest achievement is, without doubt, his non-violent struggle against injustice" (*Ibid.*, p. 9). He opines, "King's practice of non-violence was never separate from his philosophical message of love and justice. His review and reconstruction of Christian love, as a strong argument for the emancipation of blacks, gave support to his integrationist principle of non-violent revolution. He challenged the social and political injustice of American society with ideas and values that met the demands of contemporary humanism and inclusive emancipation" (*Ibid.*, p. 9).

King stood for love, justice and racial equality (*Ibid.*, p. 9). By using the non-violent means King involved in the struggle, states Jahanbegloo, for black emancipation and later against the economic injustice in America (*Ibid.*, p. 9). He had the dream of integrating the whites and blacks to live in perfect harmony. In a lecture on the life and thought of Martin Luther King Jr., James Cone, the Black theologian had made the following remarks (on 8/12/1989 at United Theological College,

Bengaluru). According to Cone, King was a political revolutionary as he spearheaded the civil right movement. He became a moral leader of America and he penetrated into the meaning of justice. King's concept of non-violence was based on his moral philosophy.

King was passionate as he challenged the slavery and the gross violence against the blacks and other oppressed groups. He states, as Coretta Scott King, his wife, reported, "The troubles of the world, my husband said, were due to incompleteness. Greece gave us noble philosophy and poetic insights, but her glorious cities were built on a foundation of slavery. Western civilization was also great, bequeathing to us glories of art and culture as well as the Industrial Revolution that was the beginning of material abundance for man. But it was based on injustice and colonialism and allowed its material means to outdistance spiritual ends" (Corretta Scott King, *My Life with Martin Luther King Jr.*, London: Hodder and Stoughton, 1969, p. 21). Corretta Scott King reported about Martin Luther King's Statement," "America", he said, "is a great nation, offering the world the Declaration of Independence and enormous technological advances, but it too is incomplete because it has deprived twenty two million negro men and women of life, liberty and the pursuit of happiness" (*Ibid.*, p. 21). He observes that Tower of London and West Minister Abbey were "built by exploitation of Africans and Indians and other oppressed peoples" (*Ibid.*, p. 22).

Martin Luther King stated that he received the Nobel prize on behalf of the civil right movement. In his speech after receiving the Nobel prize, he said, "I am mindful that only yesterday in Birmingham, Alabama, our children, crying out for brotherhood, were answered with fire hoses, snarling dogs, and even death. I am mindful that only yesterday in philadelphia, Mississippi, young people seeking to secure the right to vote were brutalized and murdered" (*Ibid.*, p. 26). He had an extreme form of solidarity for the cause of the blacks. He was a committed christian preacher who understood the liberative vision of Jesus and he lived for the emancipation and empowerment of the struggling and suffering humanity, the blacks of North America.

Martin Luther King was a strong and fearless leader who stood for the justice of the powerless blacks. One of the most important incident in the civil right movement was the Mrs. Rosa Parker event. It happened on 1st December, 1955 evening. She found a seat in the middle part of the bus. Some whites, on the way, get into the bus and the conductor asked her to move away. The words of conductor goes like this "you, nigger. Get to the back of the bus". Mrs. Parker looked at him and said

"No". This had led to an arrest of Mrs. Rosa Parker (Mary Drewery, *Martin Luther King*, p. 29).

The black community had decided to boycott the bus services of Montgomery on the day of Mrs. Parker's trial (*Ibid.*, p. 30). Taxies owned by blacks were arranged to transport the fellow blacks. The Boycott of buses was hundred per cent success. But the court had fined Mrs. Parker. In his speech King said that what the blacks need is nothing but freedom and justice (*Ibid.*, p. 33).

When the Black passengers boycotted the buses, 75 per cent of the loss of revenue to the bus companies and the Montgomery city line which led the bus companies to meet the black leader (*Ibid.*, p. 34). Martin had made three proposals: (1) The Negroes were to be treated with courtesy by bus drivers. (2) Bus seats should be filled up on 'first come, first served' basis. (3) On black route, negroes should be employed as drivers (*Ibid.*, p. 34). Though it was agreed by Inter-State Commerce Commission, segregation was found among Montgomery buses.

The boycott continued and Montgomery buses had lost over million dollars. The black solidarity was a great threat to whites (*Ibid.*, p. 36). Many Negros were arrested for no reasons as a vengeance against them by white regime. The whites also bombed the house of Martin on 30th Janaury, 1956 (*Ibid.*, p. 37). Even when the black community was daring to use violence against whites, he pacified them saying that God had asked us to love our enemies (*Ibid.*, p. 37).

Though the United States Supreme Court decreed that Alabama State and local laws requiring segregation on buses were unconstitutional, some judges acted as segregationalists. It is also found that the dreaded 'Ku Klux Klan' (a hateful secret society founded in 1866 to frighten and to lynch the blacks) came out to the street to threaten the blacks (*Ibid.*, p. 43). The decree against segregation in buses arrived in Montgomery in 20th December, 1956. But the atrocities against the blacks were continued in the Montgomery buses.

In a negro rally in 14th January, 1957, he made the following prayer, "Lord, I hope no-one will have to die as a result of our struggle for freedom in Montgomery. Certainly, I don't want to die. But if anyone has to die, let it be me" (*Ibid.*, p. 47).

He was a man of non-violence and argued for the rights of negroes as the president of the newly formed Southern Negro Leadership Conference (SNLC). He felt that non-violence was the right way (*Ibid.*, pp. 49-50). He was highly influenced by the teachings of Jesus and His non-violent approach, so also Gandhiji's ideals on non-violence (*Martin Luther King*, by Mary Drewery, p. 41).

In 1963 Martin had a campaign with local leaders in Birmingham, and he had given them Ten Commandments.

First of all, he set out to train his fellow blacks in the techniques of non-violence. Martin's strength lay in his insistence on Christian principles being observed by all demonstrators. Love must be shown at all costs.

'Love your enemies,' Jesus had insisted. 'Do good to those who hate you; bless who curse you; pray for those who mistreat you.' (Luke 6.27).

To this end, every demonstrator in the Birmingham campaign was asked to sign a Commitment Card, promising as follows:

> "I hereby pledge myself — my person and body — to the non-violent movement. Therefore, I will keep the following Ten Commandments:

1. Meditate daily on the teachings and life of Jesus.
2. Remember always that the non-violent movement in Birmingham seeks justice and reconciliation, not victory.
3. Walk and Talk in the manner of love, for God is love.
4. Pray daily to be used by God in order that all men might be free.
5. Sacrifice personal wishes in order that all men might be free.
6. Observe with both friend and foe the ordinary rules of courtesy.
7. Seek to perform regular service for others and for the world.
8. Refrain from the violence of fist, tongue or heart.
9. Strive to be in good spiritual and bodily health.
10. Follow the directions of the movement and of the captain on a demonstration.

The Birmingham Struggle was for appointing the blacks in better jobs and to restore the dignity of blacks from the racial discrimination. After the Birmingham movement, the whites have decided to give equal opportunities in jobs. The Civil Right movement had a struggle in Washington. It started on 28 August, 1963. He spoke to the crowd from the Abraham Lincoln Square where he had the historical speech, 'I have a dream'. He stated, "I am happy to join with you today in what will go down in history as the greatest demonstration for freedom in the history of our nation.

Five score years ago, a great American, in whose symbolic shadow we stand, signed the Emancipation Proclamation. This momentous decree came as a great beacon light of hope to millions of Negro slaves who had been seared in the flames of withering injustice. It came as a joyous daybreak to end the long night of captivity.

But one hundred years later, we must face the tragic fact that the Negro is still not free. One hundred years later, the life of the Negro is still sadly crippled by the manacles of segregation and the chains of discrimination. One hundred years later, the Negro lives on a lonely Island of poverty in the midst of a vast ocean of material prosperity. One hundred years later, the Negro is still languishing in the corners of American society and finds himself an exile in his own land. So we have come here today to dramatize an appalling condition. . . .

I say to you today, my friends, that in spite of the difficulties and frustrations of the moment, I still have a dream, it is a dream deeply rooted in the American dream.

I have a dream that one day this nation will rise up and live out the true meaning of its creed: "We hold these truths to be self-evident; that all men are created equal."

I have a dream that one day on the red hills of Georgia the sons of former slaves and the sons of former slave owners will be able to sit down together at the table of brotherhood.

I have a dream that one day even the state of Mississippi, a desert state sweltering with the heat of injustice and oppression, will be transformed into an oasis of freedom and justice.

I have a dream that my four little children will one day live in a nation where they will not be judged by the colour of their skin but by the content of their character.

I have a dream today.

I have a dream that one day the state of Alabama, whose governor's lips are presently dripping with words of interposition and nullification, will be transformed into a situation where little black boys and girls will be able to join hands with little white boys and and white girls and walk together as sisters and brothers.

I have a dream today.

I have a dream that one day every valley shall be exalted, every hill and mountain shall be made low, the rough places will be made plains, and the crooked places will be made straight, and the glory of the Lord shall be revealed, and all flesh shall see it together.

This is our hope. This is the faith with which I return to the South. With this faith we will be able to hew out of the mountain of despair a stone of hope. With this faith we will be able to transform the jangling discords of our nation into a beautiful symphony of brotherhood.

With this faith we will be able to work together, to pray together, to struggle together, to go to jail together, to stand up for freedom together, knowing that we will be free one day.

This will be the day when all of God's children will be able to sing with new meaning,

> "My country, 'tis of thee,
> Sweet land of liberty,
> Of thee I sing:
> Land where my fathers died,
> Land of the Pilgrim's pride,
> From every mountainside,
> Let freedom ring."

And if America is to be a great nation this must become true:

So let freedom ring from the prodigious hill-tops of New Hamspire.
Let freedom ring from the mighty mountains of New York.
Let freedom ring from the heightening Alleghenies of Pennsylvania!
Let freedom ring from the snow-capped Rockies of Colorado!
But not only that; let freedom ring from Stone Mountain of Georgia!
Let freedom ring from Lookout Mountain of Tennessee!
Let freedom ring from every hill and mole hill of Mississippi.
From every mountainside, let freedom ring.

When we let freedom ring when we let it ring from every village and every hamlet, from every state and every city, we will be able to speed up that day when all of God's children, blackmen and whitemen, Jews and Gentiles, Protestants and Catholics, will be able to join hands and sing in the words of the old Negro spiritual, "Free at Last! Free at Last! Thank God almighty, we are free at last!"

Martin was trying to get the voting rights to the blacks so that they can move into maintstream through political sphere. The right to vote was his demand. On 2nd July, 1964, as a result of struggle of the blacks, American President Lindon Johnson signed on Civil Rights Act, where he declared that everyone (including blacks who are equal before God) have equal rights in booths, class rooms, factories, hotels, theatres and common places. It was great victory of the civil right movement. In order to attain this goal hundreds of blacks (men, women and children) sacrificed their valuable lives.

In the year 1968 April, after speaking to a group of labourers who were protesting for equal wages, he was taking rest in a hotel room in Memphis, where he was shot dead by a racist.

Conclusion

Martin Luther King Jr. stood for the cause of the black people in North America, who were marginalized and discriminated. He gave lead to their struggles which was a movement towards the liberation. He sacrificed his life for their cause. But ultimately, the civil right movement was a great success as the rights of the blacks are affirmed. His dynamic leadership had helped the blacks to have justice and equality.

CHAPTER XV

THE CRISIS OF CHRISTIAN ETHICS AS A DISCIPLINE

The Christian ethicist and Christian ethics as a discipline is in crisis. Everyone has a reservation on christian ethics as they are happy and comfortable to lead an immoral life than to follow the principles of morality. It also so happens that everyone determines their own "ethics" or way of behaviour and decision-making. If everyone determines 'what is right', that will lead to a dangerous situation. Double morality is also another severe problem. It is true that persons make decisions based on selfish interests. For them values are not important, but their selfish gains. It is also a crisis that certain moral values cannot be talked about or taught.

I. The Salient Features of Christian Ethics

The Christian ethics is a very important discipline which is a headache to peripheral spirituality and to the advocates of immorality and those who involve in inhuman acts.

(a) *Christian Ethics is a Dynamic Discipline*

Christian ethics has a revolutionary spirit. It challenges the structural evil or the systemic violence. It has an uncompromising stance against the evil. It only sides justice and never the injustices. The corruption, caste system, racial prejudices, human right violations and gender-injustices and violence against creation or nature are the evils of the society which are to be questioned. Christian ethics is not neutral or silent to the injustices. The capitalism and colonialism are being challenged by Christian ethics. The globalization and the neo-colonial tendencies and their manipulations, exploitation and oppressive spirit are vehemently criticized by Christian ethics.

Christian ethics is prophetic in nature. It is not intimidated to tell the truth, which may be found intolerant to most of the evil-doers. The evil is fostered over in our communities. Even Christians are involved in bribery, money-lending and land business (land-mafia). Christian ethics is radical as it challenges unjust practices.

(b) *Christian Ethics is a Transformative Discipline*

Christian ethics is counter-cultural in character. It looks for the total transformation or a new social order. It affirms the identity, dignity and rights of everyone, especially the marginalized. Christian ethics is non-conforming ethics. It does not conform to the unjust value system. The Greek word 'metanoia' (repentance) stands for transformation. Jesus stood for the transformation of the existing value system (e.g. racial prejudices and sabbat laws).

Vishal Mangalwadi talks about his experience in Holland. He went to a milk dairy to get milk with his friend Jan. Mangalwadi states, "we walked into the milk room and no one was there to sell the milk. I expected Jan to ring the bell, but instead he just opened the tap, put his jug under it, and filled it up. Then he reached up to a windowsill, took down a bowl full of cash, took out his wallet, put twenty guilders into the bowl, took some change, put the change in his pocket, put the bowl back, picked up his jug, and started walking. I was stunned" (Vishal Mangalwadi, *Why are We Backward?*, (second edition), New Delhi: Forward Press, 2013, p. 12).

Vishal states that Holland was built on the Bible's teaching. He continued to say, "poverty, corruption and a Hellish society are only initial fruits of sin, including covetousness and theft. The ultimate consequence of sin is eternal hell for our souls. During the previous centuries, the people of Holland responded to Bible's call to repent from sin, accept God's offer of salvation and seek God's spirit who gives spiritual new birth resulted in a morally transformed life. A life lived in the power of God's spirit results in our moral transformation. It provides the energy needed to clean up corruption in society" (*Ibid.*, p. 14).

The early mission endeavours by Serampore Trio, Basel Mission and CMS mission have stood for standing against the slavery, *sati*, caste system and stood for women education, emancipation of the slave class and the dignity and rights of the poor. They were concerned of the spiritual regeneration and social transformation. The Christian community should be an agent of transformation, but now it accommodates the evil and loses its vigour.

(c) *Christian Ethics is An Analytical Discipline*

Christian ethics as a discipline is always sensitive to what is going on in the society. It is concerned of the dynamics of the society. The issues are to be identified and respond to the issues. A proper analysis of the issue is important to have an adequate response. An inadequate or irresponsible response comes out of the improper analysis. There are structural problems involved in the issue of poverty, terrorism, sex-work and suicide, which are to be identified by the analysis in order to respond to the issues. The simple and pre-determined judgements only will mislead the persons and communities. According to Richard Niebuhr, a fitting response is the outcome of the proper anlaysis, interpretation and evaluation of the data. This is found in his book (*The Responsible Self*, Kentucky: Westministe John Knox Press, 1999. pp. 60ff).

(d) *Christian Ethics is a Reflective Discipline*

It is very essential to reflect on the issues. A proper analysis and reflection can only provide proper guidance for ethical responses or decision making. An adequate reflection will help to have a responsible, meaningful and accountable decision-making or response. It is very important to note that for every response and decisions, we are responsible, accountable and answerable to the consequences. So a proper reflection based on data and facts is inevitable. An adequate discernment and direction should be found in our reflections.

The reflections of Dr. Manmohan Singh and Amartya Sen have become eye-openers to the reality of how the demonetization (ban of 500 and 1000 Rupees notes) of the NDA Government had affected adversely the poor and powerless. Both of these eminent economists point to the fact that the poor are victimized as they struggle for employment and money. Dr. Manmohan Singh has stated that the Prime Minister (Mr. Narendra Modi) has a false notion that all cash is black money and all black money is in cash. He continues to say that unlike the poor, holders of black money have access to various forms of wealth such as land, gold and foreign exchange. To throw the millions of the poor people in disarray is a mammoth tragedy according to Dr. Singh. He argues, that the vast majority of Indians earn in cash and save in cash all legitimately. It is the fundamental duty of a democratically elected government in any sovereign nation to protect the rights and livelihood of its citizens. ("Making of a Mammoth Tragedy", *The Hindu*, December 9, 2016, p. 8). Amartya Sen has stated that the result of demonetization has been only a combination of chaos and widespread suffering rather than an orderly transition to cashless society. He also argues that there is serious job losses because of this demonetization ("Serious Job Losses are Taking Place", *The Hindu*, January 17, 2017, p. 9). About sustainable development and alleviation of poverty Amit Kapoor and Sankalp Sharma have stated, "Growth alone will not be enough but must be translated into jobs for the poor and marginalized for it to become truly inclusive" ("Still Seriously Hungry and Poor", *The Hindu*, October 31, 2016, p. 9).

There are some of the examples of ethical reflections on the basis of a proper analysis of the societal issues.

(e) *Christian Ethics is a Liberative Discipline*

Christian ethics is concerned of liberation and humanization. It is concerned of a radical restructuring of the society or a structural change. It is siding the liberation of the subaltern people. The concerns such as justice and human rights are of prime importance for Christian ethics. The oppressive structures of the empire are challenged by Christian ethics. It challenges the victimization of the poor and marginalizing of women, disabled, fisherfolk, blacks, refugees and migrants and even the third-gender. It stands for human justice, eco-justice and gender-justice. The cruelty against animals are also citicized by Christian ethics. Christian ethics is critical of what is inhuman.

The peace with justice or Kingdom of God is central to the liberation. In Nazareth manifesto (Lk. 4:16-21), Jesus stood for the liberation of the Subaltern people. An integral liberation is necessary for the total well-being of all people. Jesus was siding the poor who were oppressed by the Imperial Rome and religious hierarchy. Jesus' community was an inclusive community and it was the community of the victimized. He challenged the business mafia of the Jerusalem temple (Mt. 21:12-13). He played a messianic and prophetic role to challenge the exploitative structures of the time.

The Christian community should be concerned of social justice and it should stand for the emancipation of the poor and to form a new social order. It is very important to respond to poverty, corruption, religious fundamentalism, terrorism and injustices and human right violations of various types.

(f) *Christian Ethics is a Normative and Evaluative Discipline*

Christian ethics is a normative discipline. It is concerned of norms or standards and principles or precepts. It is important to have certain set norms or *a priori* principles for dealing general or common ethical issues. But the *a priori* rules and regulations are only helpful to an extent as they are rigid or inflexible and the role of love and humanness are ignored. It may also ignore the contextual realities. For example it is not always right to condemn abortion, as we have to consider the therapeutic abortions as a justifiable act.

The *a posteriori*-agapeic approach or an evaluative approach is needed as we have to help people who are in crises. The love, mercy and humanness play vital roles in Christian ethics. It is important to help the people who are in crisis, without legitimizing the evil. Jesus was restoring the woman who was caught in adultery by admonishing her 'sin no more' (John. 8). It is important to keep normative rules as we uphold the demands of Torah and Gospel. But it is also equally important that we have to redeem the people who are victims of sin and evil who are willing to get rid of their old path. The evaluative approach has the potential to be emancipatory and liberative to help people who are in crisis. It restores the people who are in crisis.

II. The Crisis of Christian Ethics/Ethicist

Telling the truth is a very important task, but it is difficult to tell the truth as one may be victimized. When Prophet Amos was questioning the unjust feudal structures he was chased away, as nobody wants his message as it was not smooth saying. People do like comforting words than the voice of the 'roaring lion'. Prophets like Isaiah and Jeremiah were tortured as they stood for justice. They had to undergo severe forms of suffering for their voice of discomfort and dissent.

Christian ethics as a discipline cannot be intimidated to tell the truth. It has the spirit of protest as it challenges the evil that prevail in the society. The Government machinery is against Christian ethics as it questions the policies of the government which favours the rich and powerful. The corrupt bureaucracy and the feudal structures are having hatred towards the word 'ethics'. The multi-national companies are exploiting the resources of the poor countries and they make the Third World merely consumer countries. This neo-colonial tendency is being challenged by Christian ethics so they are against this discipline. The oppressive measures of the multi-national companies and their violence on the people of the Third World, especially the dalits and tribes are condemned by Christian ethics.

The multi-national companies were trying to exploit the bouxite from the tribal habitations of Niyamgiri in Odisha. So tribal people are struggling against the exploitation (Pushkar Anand and Amit Kumar Sinha, "Protecting the Rights of Tribals", *The Hindu*, February 27, 2017, p. 9). The Narmada Valley Andolan is another struggle as the tribes and dalits are forcefully evacuated from their habitat and forcefully acquired their land. It is observed that around 56 million people are evacuated in India in the name of dams and they are not yet rehabilitated. The ethical response in the form of severe struggle against the government authorities is going on in Narmada Valley. The land struggle is also going on in Chengara (Pathanamthitta District, Kerala), to have a piece of land for their dignified survival. The government machinery is trying to struck down the struggle and challenge the ethical spirit.

The Hitlerian Nazism and fascism are also coming up everywhere, including India. The fascist forces are emerging in the name of Hinduism or Islam, though they are far away from the essence of these religions. The true religiosity should advocate love, mercy, tolerance and co-existence. Religion is not meant for animosity. It is not meant for killing each other, but to live and respect one another. Fascism tries to annihilate the other, rather than loving the other. A tolerant and anti-fascist ideology is found in Jesus Christ. He said, "love your neighbour as yourself" and "love your enemies" (LK. 10:27; Mt. 5:44). The Golden rule that Jesus gave is "so whatever you wish that men would do to you, do so to them" (Mt. 7:12). The fascists are using the ideology and religion with a political and economic motive. This is what is taking place in India. The Hindutva ideology is misusing religion with ulterior motives. They do want to wipe out minorities.

The freedom of religion and even economic freedom are being questioned. The education is also directed from a fundamentalist perspective. What should be the response of ethics and the ethicists? Should we respond or we should be silent? When Hitler had his torture over the powerless, Dietrich Bonhoeffer, the German theologian and ethicist called him the anti-Christ. But the Nazi rule under the cruel monster Adolf Hitler had executed Bonhoeffer. If an ethicist is not responding to the demonic forces, he or she cannot be an ethicist. But fear is a human tragedy, and it will withdraw us from any strong response. Neutrality and irresponsibility are not related to Christian ethics.

The German Pastor Martin Niemoller has said, "In Germany, the Nazis came first for the communists, and I did not speak up because I was not a communist. Then they came for the Jews, and I did not speak up because I was not a jew. Then they came for the trade unionist, and I did not speak up because I was not a trade unionist. Then they came for Catholics, and I was a Protestant and so I didn't speak up. Then they came to me, and by that time, there was no one to speak for anyone." When things go worse, and they go out of our hands there is no way to protest evil. A responsible response is a timely action. The evil will prevail, if we are silent and neutral.

Swimming against the tides is what an ethicist has to do. In the context of evil and injustice what should be our response. It is an ethical dilemma. There can be withdrawal from the society, choosing alternative ways or responding to them without intimidation in a prophetic sense. The Qumran community had "withdrawn" from the society as they found that the world is evil and corrupt. The Hippie movement had begun as a counter-culture. They were against war, especially America's cruelty against the poor country like Vietnam. They protested against the violent policies of United States. Their slogan was 'flowers instead of guns'. By growing hair and singing songs, the Hippies had wandered everywhere to declare their dissent (But later, Hippies became victims of Narcotic addiction).

The political ethics is very strongly questioning the structural evil. The prophetic dimension is explored by Christian ethics against corruption, systemic violence and injustices. The liberative, humanizing, emancipatory and empowering process is Biblical, ethical and they are integral to the Kingdom of God. The Christian community is entrusted with the responsibility to challenge evil and to involve in the process of liberation. What happens is that the Christian churches are becoming the agents of prosperity theology and peripheral spirituality. They fail to advocate for God's preferential option for the poor. Most of the present Christian communities are siding the rich and injustices. But it is a hope that there are churches which are prophetic in nature as they roar against injustices.

Reinhold Niebuhr stated that Jesus' ethics is an ethics of love (The norm is agape), but it is also paradoxical as it is an 'impossible possibility'. This is, for him, very true with the sermon on the mount. He must have meditated on the crises in Christian ethics as an ethicist. The socialistic ideology of communism is a fascination for many, but what about the fascist face and the atheism it advocates for. For Karl Marx, religion is the opiate of the people. This is true only to an extent as religion is reduced to be inhuman. But religious communities have also contributed so much for the welfare of the dehumanized people. The positive pole (as Aloysius pieris states) of religion is that it has to do with is good and humane. Communism has become an oppressor to Christians in Soviet Russia, Communist China and Romania. How can we support the Communism which has acquired forcefully the lands of farmers in Nandigram and Singur (West Bengal) for the sake of special economic zone. The political party which was meant as pro-poor party became the pro-rich party.

We would like to follow the ethical vision which upholds the eco-justice, gender-justice and human rights of all people, especially the victimized one. But our churches are silent and opposing to these concerns. Keeping all the inhuman practices like inequality and discrimination against women, poor, dalits and other subaltern groups, they come together to pray and worship. This is the paradox and the crises we confront.

How can we support a party and its leader which involved in the Godhra Carnage which killed and tortured thousands of innocents. It is also impossible to support them as they involve in the demolition of Babri-masjid in Ayodhya. There are also inhuman acts by the pseudo-secular forces. These acts are anti-democratic, anti-secular and anti-human. The demolition leads to demonetization. These are to crush the minorities and the poor. But regret to say that many people are voting these forces to power. It is, indeed, a crises as people have lost the sense of ethics. The people are carried away by emotional aspect of religions.

The church should be pro-poor, but it happened to be anti-poor. The place of the poor is in question. The church should be an open community where all poor are to be integrated. The dominant groups are not recognizing the identity, status and rights of the people from the lower strata of the society. If they deny the status of poor, what is the ethics of the Christian community? It is also important to know, on which foundation church is built as Jesus was having the solidarity with the poor and powerless (Lk. 4:16-21). Jesus challenged the pyramidal, hierarchical, colonial and dominant structures and undergirded the disempowered. Jesus' ethics was deconstructive and decolonizing. Gandhiji was quite disappointed as he saw the discriminative attitude of the whites against the blacks as he understood that this practice has kept Christianity apart from Christ's teaching.

The rich are holding a large amount of wealth in the form of money and holdings including the land. The rich Christians are also having the selfish interests as they do not want to share, but to accumulate more. For that purpose, they are supporting the prosperity theology. The prayers and worship are meant for getting more wealth, and people use all short-cuts to have it. Instead of the 'Koinonia' or the sharing of the resources, they have the colonial spirit. The colonial spirit is used by the rich to support their exploitative and oppressive mind to accumulate wealth than to share. The blessing from God is understood by them as material prosperity and living in luxury is understood as a blessing. These are all misunderstanding as material prosperity is not necessarily a blessing. The wealth is not the sign of the elect. We are somehow carried away by the Baalism which supports fertility. It is to be kept in mind that there are just and unjust means by which one can have wealth. It is unethical if we are not sharing our resources knowing that it is God's gift.

A major crisis which Christian ethics face is the double morality. The morality we talk goes against what we do. The opportunism and ethics of convenience are common among Christians and non-Christians. Jesus was criticizing the Pharisees for their double morality. Jesus said about Pharisees, "so practise and observe whatever they tell you, but not what they do; for they preach but do not practise" (Mt. 23:3). What we believe and declare, and what we practise should go together. Belief and behaviour are to be integrally related.

Our faith and praxis are to be closely related. We claim that we believe in God, but whether we have love and concern for others. Apostle James was challenging the Christian community of their double morality. According to Apostle James, the faith without works or social concern is dead. He states, "what does it profit, my brethren, if a man says he has faith but has not works? Can this faith save him? If a brother or sister is ill-clad and in lack of daily food, and one of you says to them, "Go in peace, be warmed and filled, without giving them the things needed for the body, what does it profit? So faith by itself, if it has no works, is dead" (James 2:14-17). Double morality is a serious problem found in Christian communities. We talk about leading a simple life as Jesus had, but on the other we violate that principle by living in luxury. We talk about faithfulness and holiness, but involve in corruption by embezzling money and sexual immorality. Bertrand Russell, in his book '*Why I am not a Christian*'? has asked questions about double morality of Christians. According to him, the Christians are very serious on issues of sex, but they do not take seriously the embezzlement of money.

In the churches, the people who hold the steering is the rich and powerful. The poor are uncared and oppressed. The rich and powerful are enjoying all privileges and the powerless ones are kept rejected. The powerless are penalized and even ex-communicated for simple mistakes and no mistakes. The mistakes of the powerful and rich are always ignored. Victimizing the poor is a crime and it is a crime to leave alone the rich who is guilty. Here the double morality of the Christian community is found.

In the churches, the dalits, tribes, poor and the powerless women are undergoing severe struggle as their identity and dignity are not recognized. It is reported that even a haircut is denied for dalits in the Manchanabale village of Chickaballapur District in Karnataka (*The Hindu*, March 1, 2017, p. 6). The separate churches for Subalterns and non-Subalterns, and separate cementeries for different groups is always dehumanizing. The churches are failed to be the symbol of Kingdom of God as justice is denied to the powerless. This disempowering aspect of the church is also part of the double standards. There are churches which are closed to the poor class. Whether this is the kind of church which Jesus Christ had instituted? The women are also found voiceless and silenced in the church and the society. This victimization is also a double morality. God is God of the victimized, so attributing the senseless and irrational and dehumanizing elements to God is to be thoroughly questioned.

It is so happened to believe that being born in the world as a poor, dalit, tribe, women, black, transgender, or a differently abled is a great tragedy as they are denied of dignity and rights. The whole society and the authorities are for the powerful. In the book '*Abnormal*', Michel Foucault was disclosing the double morality of the society. A leper was chased away by the parents and relatives as they denied any relationship with him, the society and authorities are instead of his rehabilitation, tried to chase him away from the city. What this society and authorities are for? On what right they chased him away. What is his right and dignity? This kind of double morality and hippocratic society was condemned by Jesus as he restored the lepers and the differently abled. The Jewish society was also unconcerned of the powerless ones like lepers, blind and crippled, but Jesus did love and regard them. This other-regarding love of Jesus is also found in Francis of Assissi, a true disciple of Jesus who embraced and kissed the lepers.

The schools and colleges are playing vital role for the enlightening of the students. It is true that there are students who misbehave and become trouble-makers. They also involving in ragging and other malpractices. The habit of smoking, drinking alcohol and taking narcotics is increasing. It is so happened that the teachers also involve in discriminatory activities. There are teachers who misbehave to girl/ women students. Some teachers have discrimination against poor, dalit and tribe students. Some teachers keep grudge against some students and give less marks to students for the internal assessment. They fail them and even give zero marks so that poor, dalit or tribal students will not pass in the course or get a degree. They are doing it to make their future dim. Some teachers have favourites, so they will be given high marks though they never deserve it. The double standards of a teacher make him a tyrant. The ethics and integrity of a teacher is important here.

The major question is, "are we true to ourselves?" The pride of self is that we are innocent and away from any guilt, though we are guilty. And we do not want to accept any punishment. We are very happy to judge and to punish others. King David never had a self-realization as he did a grave sin in his life. When Prophet Nathan told his story through a parable, he was very furious by his self-righteousness to punish that man. But Nathan said to King David that this person is none other than yourself (2sam 12:1ff). Then only David realized his mistake. This kind of self-realization is inevitable to overcome the double morality.

For affirming the impartial judgement the Supreme Court had cited the judgement of Chola King Manu Needhi Chozhan. He lived and ruled in south India around 250 BC. He was the torch-bearer of the judge's work philosophy that "nobody is above the law and all are equal". "Manu Neehi Chozhan believed in "even justice towards friends and foes". One day while his son Veedhividangan was going around the city in a Chariot, a calf was crushed by its wheels. The mother of the calf watched helplessly its little one die, walked to the palace and rang the bell to get justice from the King. The King learnt about all that happened from the courtiers and order the prince, his son, to be killed in the same way the calf died, crushed under the wheels of his chariot. The King had witnessed this son die and thereby being just at all cost (*The Hindu* 2017, p. 7). We do not know whether there is overreaction in it, but the King's integrity to do justice at all costs is well known.

Conclusion

Keeping double morality is the most hateful thing. It is quite unethical if we are unjust in our attitude, decisions and actions. Fair dealing with all in all issues is essential to be ethical. Ethics never entertains the double standards, as ethics does not promote favouritism, inhumanity and injustice. The discriminations and inequalities should not be promoted. We should not be intimidated to tell the truth as Christian ethics sides the truth and justice. The travails of an ethicist or the ethical dilemma is that how one can overcome the double morality as we confront different crises. How ethics can be dynamic, liberative and evaluative in this process. There are critical situations which ethics as a discipline has to face, and it is important to respond to the issues. It is very essential to explore the implications of Christian humanism and its relevance to the church and society.

CHAPTER XVI

THE CHALLENGE OF EDUCATION AS A MEANS OF LIBERATION TODAY

Education is meant for a total transformation and it achieves its goal to a greater extent though the perspectives are changed today. Education was meant for change and enlightenment. It was meant to bring transformation and liberation, that is, leading people from darkness to light. Education is meant for formation, reformation, transformation and liberation. All these are interrelated. An exploration into these ideas are very important in the context of theological education.

Education and Formation

The word 'education' comes from the Latin word 'educare' means draws out. It is certainly a liberative exercise. Drawing us from darkness to light is what is enlightenment. It is movement from '*avidya*' to '*vidya*'. This enlightenment should lead us to proper formation and commitment in early Indian education system (*Gurukula*), the formation includes academic (philosophical/theological) formation and character formation. Later on the latter was given less important as congnitive or intellectual knowledge was given prominence. The spiritual and moral aspects are ignored or neglected by the present modern education system. The modern education is based on imparting knowledge or information and competition. It has arranged competitive examinations and communicates that success is only through competition. Students are forced to mug up the text books to compete in the examination. It also resulted in making education a commercial enterprise. The coaching centres are making lot of money by exploiting the students and parents. In this process the role of englihtenment and formation is lost.

Engineering and medical colleges are mushrooming as falcons in order to economically exploit the students. The investors are behind the institutions for higher education, and their focus is to make maximum profit out of them. The spiritual and ethical formation are not possible with the institutions that are founded by unethical means. A large amount has to be remitted by students in the form of capitation and tution fees in private engineering colleges and medical colleges. Here the most affected ones are the marginated as money matters in education, including theological education.

Theological education stresses the theological formation (academic), the spiritual/character formation and the ministerial formation (practical dimensions/application). Theological education should not be based on theory; but the theory and praxis should go together. Dietrich Bonhoeffer talks about formation as Christ is forming in us. It is Christ-formation. This theological formation has inspired him to challenge the unjust structures. It has political or praxiological dimensions as he opposed the policies of Adolf Hitler and called him 'Anti-Christ', which resulted in Bonhoeffer's martyrdom. The challenges involved in formation is very clear in Bonhoeffer. The formation is in question today as there are cases of clergy and laity involved corruption and immoral activities.

Education should move to the grassroots level as against today's educational system that caters the elites of the society. Education is a commercial enterprise today than a space for formation and transformation. Re-imagining education is an essential aspect today, as education should be an emancipatory exercise to liberate the poor and marginalized. Education can be formal and non-formal. Education should impart not only knowledge but also to inculcate a value system. It is also important to identify and recognize the value system of different communities and cultures, and also to convey what is counter-cultural in the context of what is evil. The prophetic value system is counter-cultural. Jesus' ethics was also deconstructive and counter-cultural.

Our behaviour and innate character are important, but it should not be mere behaviourism (B.F. Skinner was a proponent of behaviourism). According to Bede Griffiths "behaviourism, for instance, is a serious attempt to reduce the human psyche to the status of a machine by analysing it in terms of external behaviour" (*A Vision of Reality*, London: Collins, 1989. p. 277). Outward behaviour and innate attitude are to undergo the formation and transformation.

In 'pedagogy of the oppressed' Paulo Friere compares education without giving chance to students to think, and to listen and to be obediently learn as 'banking system', and the act of permitting the students to contextually think as 'dialogue'. Education has to bring formation, reformation and transformation or liberation to the disempowered and it should enlighten them in an integral way. Education is a humanizing process. If the enlightenment and liberation of the poor and marginalized is not the focus of education, the focus of education does not come to any realization.

Education and Reformation

The reformation in Christianity has taken place 500 years ago as it reformed the Christian Church from the irrational and superstitious practices like sales of indulgence, veneration of relics and saints, the papal infallibility, the extreme authority of clergy over laity and confining Bible and its interpretation of the clergy.

The missionary organizations like Basel Mission, London Missionary Society, Church Mission Society, Tranquebar Mission, and Serampore Mission have given utmost importance to education, especially the education of the slave class. Vocational training centres were started to equip the poor students of different skills. The missionaries have realized that education is a key factor for the upliftment of the poor and marginalized.

Reformation was a protest against the evil practices prevailed in the Curch. The Bible is translated into German by Martin Luther to educate the people the reformative doctrines and people's right to interpret the Bible is affirmed by him, so also the priesthood of believers. Martin Luther, John Calvin, Zwingli and Philip Melanchthom were educating the people through the reformative principles which spread as a fire against the irrational practices prevailed in the Catholic Church and the society.

The church and society in Europe were reformed radically by education through preaching and writing. Education is to conscientize the people and mobilizing the people to protest against the unjust elements. Education is not only through the formal way (schools and colleges), but also through speeches, writings and through different electronic media. It was taking places through coffee houses (pub/ public houses) in Europe and the tea shops in India.

Dr. B.R. Ambedkar emphasized the education, agitation and the liberation. Sree Narayana Guru in Kerala had inspired his followers for liberation through education. Most of the reformers had given importance to formal and informal education by which the reformation is possible. Education should have the ethical content, than making moral education separate. Integrating the moral content to all courses is important for reforming the people and structures. In India, the social evils like caste system, Devadasi system, slavery and gender discriminations were questioned by different reform movements.

Education and Transformation/Liberation

Education is a means to total transformation or liberation. It depends on what education one gives to the people, as certain education system keeps pupils as puppets or objects as it never encourage to use the critical faculty for a creative exercise. It is important to know how the education affects the life of the people. Is there anything life-changing in the education or education system?

Education should be formal and informal and it should not be a one sided exercise, but learning from one another and from the varieties of life and experience of people. What happens in education today is that we impose things on others what we think as best. But that may not be best and useful, but students are forced to study all these for the sake of degrees and employment.

It is significant to know how the present education system affects the marginated and people in the grassroots level. As Paulo Friere states, we have to get rid of the banking system, that is, forcefully trying to deposit our knowledge on others. Education should be emanicipatory and liberative. For the Christian missionaries, education was a tool to uplift and emancipate the poor and marginated. Free education for the slave class, or the slave caste, schools for women, hostels for the marginated, and free education and reservation for the poor and marginated in the colleges were the important focus of these missionaries. This is found in Basel Mission, CMS Mission, LMS Missions, Tranquebar Mission and Serampore Mission. The liberation through education was given foremost importance by them. Their mission was concrete, humanistic and liberative as they aim at the holistic transformation. It is important to explore in what way we are involving in the liberation of the marginated through our task of education? In the present education system, the money, intellect and social background play vital role than compassion and liberative dimension.

The Serampore Trio (William Carey, Joshua Marshman, William Ward) had contributed a lot to education, which resulted in the transformation and liberation of people. They studied the religion and culture which includes the linguistic studies and societal analysis. William Carey was also interested in the study of nature or the environment. They stood against caste system, *Sati*, infanticide and promoted intercaste marriages and also the education. The Serampore College was started with an integrative vision of relating the secular and sacred. The art, science and theology were offered by the college.

Translating the Bible into different languages is also an enlightening and liberative process. Understanding the divine revelation is also an important means of education. Hannah Marshman stared school for the education of women so that they may be brought to the main stream of the society. In the educative process, the teaching, the preaching (speeches) and the writing (printing — William Ward was the printer) had significant roles to play in the Serampore Mission. Serampore College was started in 1818 by the decree of Danish Charter to aim at the education of the people of India, and later the Senate Serampore College continued the ministry of theological education by the Bengal Act, 1918. In this year 2018, they celebrate their bi-centenary and centenary respectively.

The Christian missions had started schools and college for the education of the natives. They had challenged the evil social systems and provided newspapers, texts books, grammar books and sacred scriptures in order to educate them. Bible was translated into around 39 languages or dialects.

Education should conscientize and reform the people. Intellectually, socially and ethically, the people are to be reformed. It is important to discern what is right and what is wrong, through our education. According to Soren Kierkegaard, "to exist as a human being means to exist ethically." Our education, our personal life and corporate life are to be reformed. It is also important that our structure has to be radically reformed.

The reformation under the leadership of Martin Luther has re-formed or re-shaped the people by re-educating or de-educating the people. The irrational and superstitious beliefs and rituals were at play in those days which were challenged radically by the reformers. They formed a new ideology to make people think critically about the existing systems. It was re-imagination and epistemological shift in understanding. Reformation is anti-pyramidal, anti-structural and people-centred in nature. Bible was given in the language of the people and they interpreted the Bible which was a revolutionary element in the reformation. It educated the people in a new way which re-shaped their perspectives.

The transformation and liberation are the foremost elements for radical restructuring which is deconstructive. Education has an important role to play in radical transformation or liberation. It is a dynamic process which should be holistic and even revolutionary. Today's education system as in the old are mostly *status quoic* or stagnant type. It is a repetition of knowledge which is traditional, and epistemological shift is not taking place. What we need is a innovative and revolutionary dimension in education.

Jesus' discourses and ideological thrust were disturbing to the dominant groups and the Jewish rabbis of the time as Jesus questions the *status quoic* and inhuman understanding of the time. The prophetic teachings were a challenge to the existing knowledge and systems of the time. Innovative, creative and critical aspect of knowledge is not having acceptance to the existing *status quoic* structures. The dominant communities are hindering the liberation of the marginalized communities by controlling the knowledge system. They either hide the liberative knowledge which is critical or inculcate false knowledge. The Brahminic forces were countered by the sramanic forces as the non-Brahminic communities had no access to vedic knowledge and their (sramanic) knowledge and ideologies were not accepted by them. The Lokayata, the Charvaka philosophical systems and the later developed Jainist and Buddhist systems were a protest and challenge to the Brahminic understanding and knowledge. It was an epistemological shift.

The post-modern philosophy has deconstructed the existing understanding, knowledge and interpretations. Derrida and Foucault have challenged the existing parameters of knowledge which was promoted by the dominant. They stood for the decentralization of knowledge and power. When knowledge is kept hidden and controlled by the powerful, the education will not take place. Education should be an open system, as today the knowledge is available to everyone through internet facilities. But that too is available to the dominant groups. The purposeful education should enlighten and liberate the people. The *status quoic* system of knowledge were challenged by Socrates, and he became a headache to the authorities. He was teaching the students to ask questions to the existing systems which are corrupt.

Today, the so called best and Western education is only available to the wealthy class. After that education, they became the bureaucratic group who manipulate all systems for their benefits. The possibility of best and higher education for the poor is minimal and they receive only the crumbs. In the Indian education system, the condition and prospects of the poor and marginalized is pathetic. It does not cater the needs of the subaltern groups and leaving many marginalized as hopeless and helpless.

Most of the educational system (curriculum) follows in India is either Western or hybrid (combination of Indian and Western). Though we are romantic about post-colonialism (indigeneity and contextualization), the education system is still Western (the Western syllabus, books and language (English) are used and for name sake one section or a sub-section will deal with Indian). The education system that exists today is elitistic and it is meant for the brilliant ones, and not for the poor and powerless. The missionary vision of education was to emancipate the economic and socially poor but the educational institutions run by the Christians are highly commercialized. They aim at making profit with a capitalistic outlook. No pure Indian educational system is developed even in this post-colonial era with a concern for the liberation of subaltern people.

Conclusion

Education is a process of enlightening the people to acquire knowledge and it opens the minds of the people to think and act with humanity. Education should aim at humanizing people in order that they may be liberated from the irrationality, superstition and ignorance. It should enable the people to affirm the identity, dignity and rights. This is very important in relation to the poor and marginalized. Education has to reform, transform and liberate the people in an integral way. Education should be life-changing and it has to radically and dynamically bring changes in our structure and relationships. Education is to challenge what is evil, and to affirm what is humane. Education has to be meant for the emancipation of the subaltern like dalits, tribes, victimized woman and other neglected people.

BIBLIOGRAPHY

Bright, John, *A History of Israel*, London: SCM Press, 1982.

Bruce, F.F., *This is that,* Carlisle: Paternoster Press, 1968.

Clements, R.E., *Prophecy and Covenant*, Oregon: Wipf and Stock Publishers, 2009.

Harrison, R.K., *OT Introduction*, Leicester: IVP, 1970.

Jacob, E., *Theology of the Old Testament*, New York: Harper & Row, 1955.

Lindblom. J., *Prophecy in Ancient Israel*, Oxford: Basil Blackwell, 1962.

Mott, Stephen C., *Biblical Ethics and Social Change*, New York: Oxford University Press, 1982.

Muilenburg, James, *Way of Israel: Biblical Faith and Ethics*, New York: Harper Collins Publishers, 1983.

Rowley, H.H., *The Servant of the Lord and Other Essays on the OT*, London: Lutherworth Press, 1952.

Samuel, Vinay and Sugden, Chris, "Social Justice: Biblical and Practical," *Traci Journal.*

Sider, Ronald, *Rich Christians in the Age of Hunger*, New York: Hodder & Stoughton, 1973.

Von Rad, Gerhard, *OT Theology*, Vols. I & II, Edinburg : Oliver & Boyd, 1962, p. 65.

Wright, Christopher J.H., *Living as People of God*, London: IVP, 1983.

Young, E.J., *My Servant the Prophets*, Michigan: Wim Eerdmans Published, 1974.

INDEX